How to Get Inside Someone's Mind and Stay There

How to Get Inside Someone's Mind and Stay There

The Small Business Owner's Guide to Content Marketing and Effective Message Creation

Jacky Fitt, FRSA

BEP BUSINESS EXPERT PRESS

First published in 2018 by
Business Expert Press, LLC
222 East 46th Street, New York, NY 10017
www.businessexpertpress.com

ISBN-13: 978-1-94819-845-5 (paperback)
ISBN-13: 978-1-94819-846-2 (e-book)

Business Expert Press Entrepreneurship and Small Business Management Collection

Collection ISSN: 1946-5653 (print)
Collection ISSN: 1946-5661 (electronic)

Cover and interior design by S4Carlisle Publishing Services Private Ltd., Chennai, India

First edition: 2018

10 9 8 7 6 5 4 3 2 1

Printed in the United States of America.

Dedication

For Thomas, Phoebe, and Esmée

Abstract

Exploring and demystifying content marketing and providing proven and practical strategies for promotion and profit, *How to Get Inside Someone's Mind and Stay There* is for business owners, managers, and anyone with a need to market a product, a service, or even themselves!

In this book, you will learn:

- How to identify your ideal customer
- How to identify and create your key marketing messages
- The right way to be remembered
- How to write for impact, engagement, and action.

The book supplies you with all the tools you need to build and benefit your business in person, in print, and online and helps you become your sector's go-to brand of choice.

What readers say:

"An absolute gem for business owners."—Andi Lonnen

"It completely changes your way of thinking . . ."—The Book Bag

"Quite excellent, and sets the standard in this marketing genre." —Ross H

"It's the most helpful book about copywriting, digital marketing, and basically everything!!"—Good Reads

Keywords

advertising, brand, business, content, copywriting, marketing, online, PR, profit, sales, writing

There are people who make things happen.
There are people who watch things happen.
There are people who wonder what happened! Which are you?

To be successful you need to be a person who makes things happen.
—Jim Lovell, Apollo astronaut

Contents

Acknowledgments

My thanks go to Ned Hoste for his encouragement and guidance; I don't think you could find a calmer, more generous, or kinder colleague and friend.

My grateful thanks also go to my husband, Thomas, for his unwavering love and friendship, together with Phoebe and Esmée, who bring joy, love, and complete clarity to everything I do. Thanks also go to the superb Sally Ann, Mum, and Dad. Finally, my thanks must also go to all my clients, colleagues, and business associates, without whom this book would not have been written, and the team at Business Expert Press for their expertise and support.

What Is This Book Going to Do for You?

This book is your starter guide to content marketing.

Focusing on content creation and management, it delivers the fundamentals of brand awareness, strategy, and message creation to help you build a profitable business.

What Is Content Marketing?

Content marketing is the creation and delivery of relevant and valuable information by businesses to help them stand out, influence, and engage more customers—all with the aim of increasing profit.

Is it new? No, it's not. Smart businesses have been using ways to get to know and keep hold of good customers by giving them information, advice, and support for years, and it works. With the arrival of the Internet and fast digital printing, the delivery of content is changing, but people's desire for useful content has not.

How does it differ from direct marketing? Content marketing differs simply in approach; where direct marketing is the "direct" approach, for example, ads and mail-outs sent directly to recipients requesting action, content marketing concentrates on engagement first: making valuable information available to people that are looking for it, can benefit by it, and will change their habits as a result—often producing more long-term, loyal customers as a result.

Rather than banging on the doors of our customers and demanding notice, content marketing is about growing your profit through being found, befriended, and invited in.

The real fact of the matter is that nobody reads ads. People read what interests them. Sometimes it's an ad.

—Howard Gossage

Why now? Today, we have more ways of getting our information to our customers than ever before. The Internet and social media mean that people are actively looking for what you offer, so what are you doing about it?

What's next? We'll look initially at who you are and how you define yourself as a business: what you offer, what makes you different, and what are your key messages. These elements are all part of your brand. And it makes no difference whether you are a sole trader or a global corporation; your brand is the key to how people will remember and engage with you, all of which is fundamental to your content marketing strategy.

We'll then look at how to identify and find the customers that will be looking for you and how you can deliver content to them using different media and good copywriting techniques. Giving your customers what they want is paramount, and you need to do this confidently to attract and engage them.

Whether you are starting out, growing, or having a well-established business, this book will help you:

- Engage more effectively with the people that matter most—your customers
- Get the most from the words you use to talk about your business
- Be recognized as more professional
- Raise your profile

and most importantly

- Boost your profit

You see an advert for a local restaurant in the paper and you're tempted. That same day a good friend tells you about another restaurant: "The food was great and the service even better. They've got an offer for this month, you can find it on their Facebook page or website and they even share recipes and their chef's top cooking tips!"

Which restaurant are you going to book?

"The most valuable real estate in the world is the corner of someone's mind."

CHAPTER 1

What's in a Brand?

Brand: n & v—n. 1a a particular make of goods. 1b an identifying trademark, label, etc., 2 a special or characteristic kind (brand of humour), 3 an identifying mark burned on livestock with a hot iron . . .
—Concise Oxford Dictionary

Today, the word *brand* in business describes so much more than the dictionary definition above. Yes, it is the name for a trademark or label, but in business a brand describes the whole "package," not just the badge; it's about what you stand for.

Successful brands make themselves attractive to people who want to engage and buy from them because they respond to the brand's primary function. This function or purpose is why the business exists; it helps shape its values and it doesn't change.

In 1925, Henry Ford placed an advertisement for his cars, which summarized his vision of "opening the highways to all mankind." These words were revisited by President and CEO Alan Mulally in 2012, as through the better use of resources, sustainability, clever design, and a positive contribution to the world, Ford still holds to that vision today and it continues to shape what they do.

People today care about the brands they buy. They want to know about their vision, history, and values, so that they can feel they are making the best buying decisions for themselves, their businesses, and, more and more today, the planet.

Knowing what your brand stands for means you'll be confident in communicating it to others as a true reflection of your business.

Your Brand Matters

The brand of a business is not simply its logo; through its function or purpose it is also:

- The quality of the product or service
- The feel of the packaging the product arrives in
- The attention to detail of the salesperson
- The speed with which your query or complaint is answered
- The language and tone of voice you use to attract your attention
- The care and support offered after you have made your purchase
- The professionalism of your website and business literature
- The work in the community of the business
- The way you and your employees behave
- You.

Simply put, a brand is a promise. By identifying and authenticating a product or service, it delivers a pledge of satisfaction and quality.
—Walter Landor[1]

And by using this promise you can build an audience, extend the reach of your engagement through effective content marketing, and grow your profits. Walter Landor again: "Products are made in the factory, but brands are created in the mind." "Nearly half of respondents (48%) want to purchase from brands that are responsive to their customers on social media."

Sprout Social Index

Today, brands have to work harder to engage their customers over and above the direct selling and traditional shop front approaches. It's important to move with the times to compete with the more nimbly minded operations that spot the emerging trends for greater engagement with

---

[1]Walter Landor is an acclaimed designer and pioneer of branding and consumer research techniques.

customers on a range of different platforms and media. That's what content marketing is all about.

> Content is an important piece in all of our marketing efforts . . . extending our messaging through content is a great way for us to continue to convert our customers.
> —Walter Frye, *Director of Entertainment Marketing and Sponsorships, American Express*

Creating shareable content is also making brands think more creatively about what their customers actually want to hear, as a route to creating greater loyalty, trust, and, ultimately, greater sales.

> Content is critical for us because it's the currency that drives our relevance and therefore consumer consideration for our brand.
> —Dan Vinh, *VP Global Marketing, Renaissance Hotels at Marriott International*

Big brands, big bucks you may think, *yet* the principles that apply to big brands, their brand behavior, and content marketing strategies are exactly the same for smaller businesses and will create greater engagement and growth as a result.

> You can't be everything to everyone but you can be something to someone.
> —Andrew Davis, *Brandscaping: Unleashing the Power of Partnerships*

No matter how small your budget, start thinking like the brand you want to be and let's begin.

CHAPTER 2

Drop the Pitch

A Short But Important Chapter

Good content marketing makes people stop and think, then do something in a different way—your way.

Imagine creating customers who look forward to receiving your content—how would that boost your brand loyalty, referrals, and profit?

Can't Buy Me Love

Now, let's be clear; content marketing is not direct selling. As we touched on right in the beginning of the book, content marketing is about engaging your customer: connecting with people who are searching for the information you are producing. They want to learn and make sound buying decisions and are, therefore, already interested in what you have to offer.

Once your customers are engaged, content marketing is about changing their behavior through consistently creating and communicating relevant and valuable information to them. Helping your customer make more intelligent choices earns their trust, and, in turn, you will be rewarded with their business and loyalty. Ultimately, you are creating not just a customer, but also an unpaid ambassador for your brand.

Turn Up the Volume

It's time to turn up the volume on what you can offer your customers. Integrated into an overarching marketing strategy, content marketing gives you greater authority within your sectors, raising your profile and the ability to attract and retain more of what matters most: loyal customers who love what you do.

CHAPTER 3

Nobody Understands Me

Think Like Your Customer

The main focus of content marketing is not the hard sell; it's to help inform your customer, and in order for it to do that, you must understand them, their needs, and their "pain," and be able to think like them. You need to tell them what they need to hear, which in general terms means consistent, valuable information relevant to their lives. Working out what you need to deliver is about **empathy** and "walking in their shoes." Because when you understand how someone feels and why—their motives for arriving at a certain set of values or opinions—you're a good way to knowing what content will interest and inspire them to take action.

Before you criticize someone, walk a mile in his shoes. That way,
when you insult them, you'll be a mile away and you'll have his shoes.
—Jack Handey

Often quoted, also true but *not*, I think you'll agree, very empathetic.

Your content marketing will be doing its job when it inspires interest and loyalty and reinforces your brand's reputation, all of which build trust. Intangible, yet important for brand profile good word of mouth and a strong reputation, brands live or die by *trust*. Good content marketing can also go a long way to repairing trust if it is damaged.

Content marketing is not new; it has been successfully used for many years. In 1895 U.S. agricultural machine manufacturers John Deere launched *The Furrow*, a magazine for farmers on how to become more profitable. It is widely regarded as the first "customer publication" and is currently read in 27 countries and in 14 languages; it's still going strong today.

The *Michelin Guide* is another early content marketing hero. Developed by the Michelin tire company in 1900, the guide was developed to give the growing number of car owners' information and tips on maintenance and travel. Why? Because Michelin had the simple aim of wanting new car owners to drive more; if they drove more miles they would need to change their tires more often. And who would they turn to when they needed new tires? To those lovely, helpful people at Michelin, of course. The *Michelin Guide* is also still going strong, and from tires to tiramisu, their early system of giving good "stop-offs" star ratings has developed into the global recognition of some of the world's best places to eat.

Focus your sights firmly on your customer: their needs, their lives, their issues; what matters to them will attract them; what attracts them and satisfies their need or desire, they will buy.

If what you are saying offers no value to your market—no insight, interest, or help, it will be ignored. If what you say is inconsistent in its quality, tone, and/or how often it appears, it can create frustration and be mistrusted. This mistrust will act upon your brand, and your investment in content marketing will, at best, be pointless and, at worst, create a bad impression.

So, it pays to do your research, plan your strategy, roll it out, and review it regularly.

You need to create content that is:

- Focused on your customers' needs
- Valuable
- Consistently delivered
- Relevant
- Accessible
- Easily found

Checking on how your competitors do things is all part of forming your plans, but don't be afraid to break away from the perceived industry "norms" by putting your personal stamp on your writing to create your own tone and style. Just as you are unique, so is your business and your brand. Delivering your messages with passion and integrity is the way to build trust. Real personality and consistency are what matter in a successful content marketing strategy. Trying to be something you're not will be a short walk to a long drop.

Be confident, be consistent, be you.

So, how do you approach your content strategy? Let's find out with the "what, who, why, how and when" of content strategy.

CHAPTER 4

What, Who, Why, How, and When?

First things first; everything we are going to look at has just one person in mind: your ideal customer. Their importance is paramount and in order to reach and appeal to them you need to be very clear about five things.

What do you offer?
Who do you offer it to?
Why should they buy from you?
How are you going to reach them?
When are you going to reach them?

What Do You Offer?

It is critical for successful content marketing that you clearly understand your product or service completely: your niche in the marketplace together with your vision, purpose, values, and goals. What you do together with the way you go about it is the basis of your brand and behavior. Your **core values** are your influencers and feed into your **core actions**, which include your unique selling points (USPs).

Core Values

Your core values are what define your behavior as a business. Bound up with your values, they are what many businesses term as *vision* and *mission statements*. Remember Henry Ford's vision in Chapter 1, the statement of intent and purpose of his business? Businesses often blend their mission (current) and vision (future) statements, as with Google, whose mission is "To organize the world's information and make it universally accessible and useful."

What are the **values** that are important to you? They may be:

- Niche expertise
- Family-run business
- Honesty and transparency
- Independence
- Commitment to the environment
- Commitment to training and emerging technology

By thinking about them and writing them down, it's much easier to refer to and remind yourself about them. Creating vision and mission statements also helps define your thoughts on direction and planning.

Core Actions

Defining your core actions or USPs will help you deliver your **values.**
They may be:

- Industry accreditation/certification
- Money-back guarantees
- Exclusive access
- Free delivery
- 24-hour support
- Extended warranties
- Cost transparency
- Personal service and aftersales care

Who Do You Offer It To?

Now consider **who** will want what you have to offer.

Core Customer

You may be a business to business (B2B) or a business to consumer (B2C) enterprise—or both—but who is your core customer? For example, is it:

- A mother of preschool children?
- A busy procurement manager?
- A small business that buys office supplies in bulk?
- A student living in Chicago?
- A growing retail business requiring shop and office refits?
- A dog lover living within a 10-mile radius of Little Rock?
- A partner in a Boston law firm experiencing a challenging change?

Create a profile for your core customer: informed by what you have to offer, it's an outline of your ideal customer and the market or sector they are in. If you have different products and services and/or industry markets, there will probably be a slightly different profile for each.

For your core or ideal customer's profile, pin down, to within a reasonable range, their:

- Gender
- Age
- Education
- Marital status
- Income

If you are selling B2B, drill down into which businesses would be looking for your products and services, including:

- Size
- Turnover
- Location
- Ambition

Add this information to their:

Values—how they like to do business?

Learning—where do they find out about things? For example, the Internet, national newspaper, industry journal, or the local corner store.

Mobile/social media habits—are they tech savvy, or do they steer clear of online engagement?

Actions—are they cautious about adopting new behavior, or are they brave "first responders"?

When you are clear about your **core values, core actions, and core customer**, you will find it easier to be clear on the problem you are solving for your customer and be able to answer the really important question: **Why should they buy from me?**

Why Should They Buy from You?

Get clear on the benefits you offer.

Think about why your core customer is likely to give you a second glance.

- Why will they benefit—what problem are you solving for them?
- What might they like or dislike?
- Do they *need* what you offer (food, shelter, etc.) or might they *want* it—is it a luxury item that they feel will enhance the quality of their life and status?

If it's a business:

- Will it help make their systems simpler, more efficient, or cheaper?
- Will it make their products, and them, work better/more attractive?

- Will it raise their status?
- Will it help fight off their competition?
- Will it give the boss or team better "life balance"?
- Will it help boost their sales?

From the information you have collated about your core or ideal customer, give them a name and a job, a family background, and their own set of aspirations for them or their business. Decide what keeps them up at night, what gets them excited, and how they like to relax. Write a "pen portrait." This handy tool means you can sense check what you create for your marketing and also help others—members of your team or a copywriter you engage—who will be creating content for you. As time goes on you should also review and update these portraits as your business and markets evolve.

If you find that there is a mismatch between your core values, core actions, and core customer—what benefits you bring and what problem you thought you were solving—retrace your steps, redo the process, and gather more evidence and research. This knowledge is fundamental to building your business successfully and for fulfilling its potential.

Now that you've identified "Todd" or "Sarah" or a particular business setup in your mind, you have a much greater chance of tapping into what really matters to them and be able to occupy a corner of theirs. This information will give you what you need to create your core messages.

Core Messages

If your business services both B2B and B2C customers, their needs may differ and overlap and you need to identify each one. Understanding what problems you are solving and establishing all the benefits you offer gives you the vital information to help shape your **core messages** and create great content to which your core customer will be attracted. For example, your core messages will help you:

- Establish a rock-solid foundation on which to base all your content
- Perfectly position you in your marketplace

- Express your values clearly
- Stand out from your competitors
- Attract the kind of customers you want

These messages feed into your brand behavior and sit at the heart of your content marketing and the strategy you use to deliver it.

Core values + Core actions + Core customer + Core messages = Content marketing strategy

How and *When* Are You Going to Reach Them?

To do its job effectively, content needs to be delivered to your customers in the way they want to receive it, when they are able to take it on board.

Within your profiling you will have looked at how your core customer likes to receive his or her information. These are the "platforms," or routes, that will work well for you. With a seemingly overwhelming array of social media platforms, people feel that they need a presence on everything. You don't. For example, if you sell accounting software and want to find and engage with accountants, you would be far better putting your energy into creating a great LinkedIn profile, joining relevant LinkedIn groups, answering questions, writing articles for industry journals, and engaging professionals who need your services than putting a lot of effort into an Instagram profile. It all depends on where your core customer looks for their information and which platforms they trust.

Will a weekly blog work for you? Possibly. For example, if you run a garden center, a weekly blog on seasonal planting and maintenance would be very appealing to gardeners. They will have a good reason to visit it regularly as the seasons demand different gardening preparations and techniques, and, as such, it will help you build a loyal following. Platforms like Twitter would enable you to give gardeners instant weather-related tips, or how about YouTube? If you produce a really versatile product, what better way to engage and show off its full potential than to literally demonstrate how good it is in short videos?

As with gardening, timing plays a role in getting the most from the content you serve up. Sending out too much can be as damaging as delivering too little. Being erratic doesn't build trust and being too pushy turns people off. The key is often to test the water, encourage feedback, ask what your customer would prefer, listen to them, watch your competitors, and learn from everyone.

According to Econsultancy and Outbrain, "More than **90%** of marketers believe that content marketing will become ever more important." Yet, "Only **38%** of brands have a defined content marketing strategy."

But you are not going to be one of them. Read on!

CHAPTER 5

Give to Get

Before we proceed, I just want to underline a very important, if not central, element of content marketing.

Think about your business culture and be honest about your attitude to the Internet and social media, your capacity to take on additional work, and the skills you have to deliver it. But most importantly:

Are You Comfortable with Giving Stuff Away?

I hope so, because that is exactly what we are about to do. It can often be counterintuitive, yet it works so well. Ancient wisdom was not wrong:

Give and it will be given to you. (Luke, Ch. 6 v38)

Can You Share Like You Mean It?

You must let your content do its job. Once you have created content you need to be alive to the different opportunities to use it. Content marketing is about sharing; sharing your valuable content with those that will find it useful and will want to share it too. So, naturally, you want to get your message to as many interested parties as possible. Offering the same information just packaged in a different way, on a different platform, or via differing resources. For example, you might use a "how to" article on your website and within a printed brochure; a press release needs to be signposted via a tweet and be found on your website; newsletters should be sent to customers, associates, and local press news desks as a matter of course. Get used to thinking creatively about your information—how you can "join up the dots" for your core customer so that they feel reassured in your confident and consistent content delivery.

So, let's continue and be prepared to give like you mean it and share in the full expectation of your generosity being returned. You won't be disappointed. If you don't like giving stuff away and think that sharing is a profitless activity, keep reading, I'm going to change your mind.

CHAPTER 6

Less Is More

Working Out Your Content Strategy

Your **content strategy** is going to deliver your **content marketing**; in other words, it's going to help you get your message out there. It's about being the best answer to your core customer's questions.

A reality check for our ideas and budget—what we *want* to create and what is *achievable* may be some way apart. In order to be effective it is better to start slowly, be consistent and build, rather than go mad, fizzle out, and squander your efforts. A written plan or strategy is very important with review dates in the diary to measure how successful your strategy is performing. If you find you have the will but not the way to create what you need, it would be worth considering outsourcing to experienced professionals. Initially you may feel in need of experienced support to help get you going, and outsourcing a part or all of your content marketing can go a long way to helping you achieve your goals.

So, what channels are there for content marketing? In no particular order, how about the following (and more)?

- Articles in specialist publications
- Websites
- Blogs
- Twitter
- Instagram
- Facebook
- YouTube
- "How to" guides
- eBooks

- Infographics
- Pinterest
- Webinars and podcasts
- "Ask us" advice forum
- Specialist group forums
- Monthly newsletters
- Face-to-face seminars and workshops
- Video guides

Most businesses cannot call on the resources of American Express or Virgin to create, oversee, and report back on content marketing activity. *Congratulations if you can and thank you for buying this book.* To achieve the all-important consistency, your strategy needs to be **aspirational** but also **manageable**.

Drawing on your core customer profiling work to establish where and how they like to receive information means you can focus on the tactical aspect of delivering your content on some key platforms. For example, bearing in mind your profiling, it may be that you decide to create a content marketing strategy around:

- Website
- Emailed newsletter
- Monthly blog
- Twitter
- LinkedIn
- Printed brochure

If you have expertise in presenting and design, then seminars, videos, and infographics would make sense. Similarly, if you are good at writing, a blog and newsletter would be a good place to start. If you have skill gaps that you know could damage your brand, it's important to work with other professionals that can support you and broadcast your key messages professionally and in line with your brand behavior. **Don't be tempted to cut corners**; it's a waste of time and money and could well damage your efforts in the long run.

Whatever your skills, *always* refer to what you know about your core customer: how they like to receive information and from where. If they feel at home on the Internet, then emails, blogs, and Facebook will give you greater profile and reach. If they don't, look at printed newsletters and advertorials; however, it's fair to say that in this day and age, websites and social media (the likes of Facebook, Instagram, and Twitter) should be used to deliver at least part of your content marketing strategy. B2B or B2C, your customers won't be using all the online or Internet-based platforms available, but I'm willing to bet that they will be using at least one or two and you need to know what that is and be there for them.

Social media in particular is changing fast. Early adopters are aging and being joined by older age groups who are now doing their searching and sharing on phones and tablets, as opposed to PCs and laptops. As of 2017 the 25–34-year-olds form the largest group of users across the majority of social platforms,[1] more of which later.

Part of creating a content management strategy is also about being aware of where your customer is, what they are watching, reading, and listening to. Publishing content on the right platform acts like an advert to generate new engagement; it's important to ensure that your content is being seen by the right people, in the right place, and at the right time and pitched in the right way to interest and influence them.

Most importantly, make it easy, make it useful, make it consistent, and when your do receive feedback or comment, *always* respond.

Talking, Listening, and Taking Note

Now, it's time to think about exactly what you are going to talk about—the ideas you'll need to create your content. To keep up the momentum for content creation, it is wise to plan at least 6 months ahead; tying your content marketing into your overarching marketing plan will mean you'll spot ways of highlighting upcoming events, innovation in your industry, community activity, and PR that can all help feed your content creation. This plan needs to stay flexible to make room for reaction to new regulation or the impact of wider events, but with a plan in place, you've got your road map that will help you stay on course.

---

[1]Statista. 2017. "Age distribution of active social media users worldwide as of 3rd quarter 2014, by platform." https://www.statista.com/statistics/274829/age-distribution-of-active-social-media-users-worldwide-by-platform/

CHAPTER 7

What Makes Us Share?

People like to share stories, ideas, tips, and opinions all the time. Having the "inside line" on a new service, product, or idea that raises our status makes us feel good. So, how do we make our core customer feel good?

We All Love to Feel Like Insiders

Most people like to feel knowledgeable, to feel they have access to useful information that others may be unaware of, and they then gain status by sharing it.

Content marketing gives you the ability to help people feel good, change how they do things, and influence others in your favor. Remember the restaurant example discussed right at the beginning of the book? Friends share information and recommend stuff all the time. Word of mouth is the "Holy Grail" for great advertising, and the swift and highly reactive social media platforms like Twitter, Facebook, Tumblr, LinkedIn, Pinterest, and Instagram are making sharing faster and spreading messages far wider than ever before.

After identifying your core customer, the person that is going to be most receptive to your content, it's also important to understand what makes them want to share information. Because when you do, and you use that knowledge, you'll understand why they have just told several of their friends about you.

We All Want to Feel Special, Intelligent, and Loved

Understanding why certain news items, videos, memes,[1] advertising campaigns, etc. become highly shareable and therefore more successful than

---

[1]A "meme" is the word used to describe an idea, a behavior, or a style that spreads throughout a culture being passed on from one person to another.

others is big business for agencies servicing big brands that are chasing even bigger profits. But it's not rocket science; it is about human behavior, and regardless of budget, you can apply the same principles to increase the reach of your content. Jonah Berger did a huge amount of research for his 2013 book *Contagious*[2] within which he looks in detail at why some things catch on, whereas others don't. In it Berger outlines six key STEPPS: social currency, triggers, emotion, public, practical value, and stories—a combination of which makes content spread like wildfire. I recommend the read if you want to dig deeper into this fascinating area. The way I have always viewed good, sharable content runs along similar lines. I have already talked about the need for all humans to feel **special**, **intelligent**, and **loved**. By helping your core customer to feel this way, you can create the greatest engagement for your business and brand.

Your customer will feel special when they take up an "exclusive" offer from you; they gain access to helpful resources others don't know about, and they have the ability to ask direct questions and get helpful information back.

Your customer will feel intelligent when they are sent great free advice, and passing it on means they in turn become a recognized source of valuable information.

Your customer will feel loved when they feel you are aware and are thinking of them, that you care about their issues and are working to make their lives easier.

Isn't that what you want from the brands you buy into?

It is no coincidence that I am writing about how you can make people feel. No decision we *ever* make is completely objective. It's impossible; from the moment we are born we make judgments and decisions based on our past and current experience of trust, betrayal, love, frustration, fear, greed, loyalty, contentment, philanthropy, education, and everything in between. Part of planning content is working out how you want your customer to *feel* about it and the emotional response you want to get back.

Don't believe me? Deep within our brains is a set of neurons called the amygdala. Part of the limbic system, this area has been pinpointed

---

[2]J. Berger. 2013. *Contagious* (New York, NY: Simon & Schuster). ISBN 978-1-47111-169-3.

by neuroscientists as governing our emotions as well as playing a role in decision making. If you want someone to make a decision, you'll need to take into account the way they will want to feel about taking that step too.

Be in no doubt; it's how people *feel* about your content that will make them relate to it, act on it, share it, or bin it.

To help your content be shared and therefore maximize your efforts, you need to ensure it combines elements of:

Value—informative, opinion-changing, useful
Currency—newsworthy, trending, influencing
Story—inspiration, vision, ideas, journey
Emotion—desire, joy, relief, envy, fear, humor

Think about the kind of things you receive and like to share and you'll find that you, along with everyone else around the world, respond to these same drivers.

In your content marketing creation, for whichever platform you choose to use, keep checking your content against these four drivers. In doing so you may also discover opportunities you are missing.

So, let's begin to create content. For this your brand needs a consistent tone and style. A "voice" that accurately reflects your businesses personality. If you are a sole trader, that is most definitely "you."

If you are a growing business with a team, it's just as important to understand and create this tone and delivery. A range of different materials and styles from one brand waters down professionalism and simply confuses customers, so work out your tone of voice and stick to it.

CHAPTER 8

Setting the Tone and Delivering the Goods

From sole traders to international corporations, content marketing is a great tool for creating loyal customers and growing profits. It is part of doing business today, and **there has never been a more important time to write well**.

Dictated by your ideal or core customer's tastes, you need to work out the right tone of voice for your brand. Essentially, through this tone of voice your brand will build a "personality" that your customer can relate to. We all want to feel confident and secure in our choices, and that's how you want your customer to feel about buying from you. You are the "safe pair of hands" or the "maverick"—whichever appeals to them, that's what you need to be.

If your core customer is, say, an HR executive, do you think they would respond well to a style of writing that was overly familiar, irreverent, and full of urban slang? It's hardly going to project your professionalism, expertise, and abilities. If, however, your core customer is a teenage boy, you'd probably be on much firmer ground and enjoy far greater engagement. If you do want to engage the youth market, a word of advice: Keep it authentic. There is nothing more excruciating than an adult using what they believe is "teen speak" to talk to young people. Get either reliable advice at source or an extremely competent professional writer. And while being too familiar has its drawbacks, so does appearing too cold and distant.

Referring to your business or brand in the third person will always create an immediate barrier between you and your reader; for example, "Acorn Fabrications are the market leaders in carbon fibre." That's all well and good if it's a statement made by someone external to the business, but it stands out as disengaged and cold on the company's own website, or within their brochures. Using the first and second person, "we," "us," and "our," "you" and "your," is not, as some people claim, too informal. It's simply the best way to communicate directly and respectfully with someone you'd like to get to know better. You wouldn't use the third person when you talk to someone face to face, so don't use it when you write.

Remember: we all want to feel special, intelligent, and loved.

It's also important to have one or two people responsible for the content output. Too many writers have the potential to wreak havoc with tone of voice, and it often means many hours of editing and can negate any advantage of consistent output. To avoid this, ensure that just one or two well-briefed people curate your content. This may be you and an assistant or two members of your team. Remember you're building trust; inconsistent writing styles from one article, web page, guide, or blog to the next will only promote confusion in your readers—it will erode trust rather than build it.

On the whole, people are lazy. And that's good for you because this means they want quick and easy solutions to their problems—they like consistency and valuable information because it builds their trust and gives them the confidence to buy from you without having to trawl around for better offers. So, next we are going to look at different ways to deliver your content and the art of good storytelling and confident copywriting.

CHAPTER 9

The Long and Short of It

How much is too much or not enough?

So the writer who breeds more words than he needs, is making a chore for the reader who reads.

—Dr. Seuss

With the advent of Twitter and its initial 140, and more recently extended 280, character allowance; the 60-second "how to" video; and elevator pitches demanding that we become concise in our communication, you'd be forgiven for thinking that you need to keep all your messages short and snappy whatever you're doing. I disagree; **there's a need for both long and short copy; it all depends on the job they are required to do.**

Millions of people use Google, Yahoo, Bing, etc. every day because when they want to find something, they **search** for it first, and they are very, very unlikely to come across listings of tweets or Facebook posts. Try it yourself: Type "gardening equipment" into Google search and see how many YouTube videos, Facebook pages, Instagram posts, or tweets come up on the first page. There won't be any.

More and more, the search engine spiders' job (spider is the name given to the automated systems that unrelentingly check and index content on websites) is to give searchers lists of online resources that offer relevant and valuable content as close to the words they have typed into the search box as possible. We'll be looking at how you can get them doing a good job for your online content or website a little later on.

In his book *Ogilvy on Advertising*[1] and writing before the dizzying rise of the Internet, advertising legend David Ogilvy, firmly believed

---

[1]D. Ogilvy. 2009. *Ogilvy on Advertising* (London: Prion). Reprinted ISBN 978-1-85375-615-3.

that long copy suggests that you have something important to say and demonstrates expertise.

Now, **this is not to be confused** with a mass of copy that is full of poorly written hyperbole, repetition, and waffle. Long copy demands good copywriting skills and, done well, more often than not leads to greater conversion and sales. David Ogilvy again: "The more facts you tell, the more you sell." And not simply facts but also emotion—giving us more reasons to read on, engage, and ultimately buy.

In direct sales split tests, where long and short copy were compared, the long invariably outsells the short. The reasons for this are based in human behavior. People like to be informed. They want to learn about something that catches their interest and they like passing this information on. Remember special, intelligent, and loved.

Short-form copy or storytelling **is** very important in today's social media world. It is a highly effective way of attracting attention, of "signposting" the main event. When you have someone's attention, you need to back it up with the right content in the right place, and more often than not, long copy "outpulls" or outsells short copy every time.

So, as we begin to explore the different platforms and channels, bear in mind what's going to work well for you and how flexible you can be in your approach to delivering great content to the person that matters most: your core customer. Research has been done on optimum lengths for the best results on social media sharing, more of which in Chapter 19.

Finally, ensure you measure the results of your content marketing, and do it regularly. This may be through free analytics software such as Google Analytics on your website, which highlights visitor activities: the content they view, the pages they like, the blogs they prefer, and the pages from which they exit your site. Watch the rise in followers on Twitter, engagement from emails, sign-up forms for exclusive offers, a rise in contacts via LinkedIn, and inquiries following newsletters. Look for patterns and what platform works better than another. Give it time, it's not a sprint, but if you are using something that no one is responding to, don't ignore the signs. Dump it and explore other platforms or routes.

CHAPTER 10

Sticky Straplines

What Are They?

The strapline, or tagline, is a collection of words that accompany a company's logo or name. An important "touchstone" for a brand, the creation of a strapline often comes out of the initial branding process but not always, and if your brand doesn't have one, it's an opportunity missed. Some people think straplines are old fashioned (their origins date back to the advent of mass manufacturing in the late 1800s), but just ask a child to reel off a few of their favorite products' straplines and you'll see just how powerful they remain.

Why Use Them?

As an essential part of creating effective content marketing, defining your core values, actions, and messages should include looking at how you are already describing your brand and give you an opportunity to refine your strapline or create one.

Defining for your core customer *why* they need you, straplines can articulate ambition and personal progress and offer exclusivity, status, and practical benefits. The perfect sound bite, a strong strapline is really useful as part of your content strategy. An "aide-memoire" for online and offline material, you can use it on printed material, as an introduction or sign-off to a blog, newsletter, or email; on websites; vehicles; and ads, the idea being that people will associate that message with your brand.

Does exactly what it says on the tin.

—Ronseal

Let's look at a selection of historic and current straplines and why they work: HSBC wants you to think of it as, "The world's local bank"; Zanussi sees itself as, "The appliance of science." Every one of a certain age remembers "Beanz Meanz Heinz" and the seductive "Liquid engineering" from the makers of engine oil Castrol GTX. And that's what it's all about: creating a memorable signpost to your brand, identifying certain words and feelings (remember our decisions are all driven by these) with your business and brand that trigger a response.

The Anatomy of the Strapline

What should you think about when you begin the process to create or refine your strapline? Using the work you have done on your core values, actions, and messages, form your ideas around the following strapline guidelines:

Keep it simple. Fewer than five words of one syllable each is a good goal.

Just do it
—Nike

Make it meaningful to your core customer. Make it positive, even emotive, showing off the benefits of the product or service for them.

Because you're worth it
—L'Oréal

Be honest. Don't promise the world; be respected for being real.

We try harder
—Avis

Give the benefits. Try and project how using the product or service will benefit either your core customer's quality of life or status.

Melt in your mouth not in your hand
—M&M's

Be original. Human brains like alliteration and rhymes. But be careful: Simply firing off three words that happen to have the same initial letter is often (but not always) a lazy answer. Think about what you actually do.

> You shop, we drop
> —Tesco Home Delivery

Give it personality and confidence. Make it your own. Make it fun and therefore memorable.

> American by birth, rebel by choice
> —Harley Davidson Motor Company

The following strapline was reputedly seen advertising an all-Asian building company in London: "You've had the cowboys, now meet the Indians." Along with another gem from a firm of undertakers: "We're the last people to let you down."

Bigger brands also display a confident take on the approach to life and aspirations of their target market:

> Think different
> —Apple

Creating the perfect strapline can be tough, and, for one reason or another, plenty of organizations get it wrong. The strapline may be too ambiguous, lengthy, or bizarre so that nobody can relate to it or remember it, thus missing the point entirely. It also may be just dull end empty; the use of clichés like "working together" or the word "solutions" is particularly lazy and generic so try and avoid these.

To craft a great strapline, use what you know about your core customer and . . .

- Keep it simple
- Make it meaningful

- Be honest
- Give the benefits
- Be original
- Project personality

There's one very famous exception to the simplicity rule—isn't there always? No one knew what it meant, but it sounded important, technical, and mysterious. People loved saying it because it made them sound knowledgeable. Loosely translated from the German as "advancement through technology," it's also a good example of a big brand's confidence and has stood the test of time.

Vorsprung Durch Technik

—Audi

A year or so ago I was commissioned to create a strapline for a care business that provided personal care to people, either elderly or those with mobility issues, who wanted to live independently at home. Already successful and well established in their part of the country, the strapline they had created was, in fact, more of a mission statement:

Friendly reliable care in your own home in York and Selby

It was accurate and showed their intention, but it wasn't memorable; it didn't easily trip off the tongue, or convey emotional safety. In short, it didn't appeal to their core customer, and it didn't really appeal very much to the business or the careers they employed either.

I wanted to get to the bottom of what their core customer wanted. What was the most important thing to them? What would allay their fears and make them take notice of the service? I came up with a new strapline:

Live happily at home

Why Does It Work?

It is simple.

It is meaningful—speaking directly to its core customer; it's what they want and is therefore desirable and memorable.

It is honest—it's the "why" of the business model and the aim for all its clients.

It projects the benefits of the business's work.

It is original and stands out in their marketplace.

It projects personality and emotion—safety and comfort.

The care company loved it, their clients remember and respond to it, and their competitors are still trying to match it.

Finally, live with it before you go live with it. When creating straplines it is important to "live" with it for a while. Give it some time to percolate. You may discover that you have missed a vital point, someone else may have beaten you to it, or, in the end, it just doesn't say what you need it to. Test it on trusted associates and long-term clients and respect and value their feedback.

CHAPTER 11

The Business Card

Starting the Conversation

What Are They?

Small, compact, and stubbornly resisting the digital onslaught, the business card has been around in one form or another since the 16th century in Europe and is an internationally recognized way of quickly trading key contact information about the person you're meeting and their business.

> *It ain't what they call you, it's what you answer to.*
> —W. C. Fields

For B2B and B2C face-to-face meetings the business card is usually the first physical content transaction, so why do so many of us fail to see or use its full potential?

Why Use Them?

The business card is still around because it works. Largely of a standard size to fit easily into wallets—we've probably all come across the larger ones and on the whole found them really irritating—how should we approach this content marketing stalwart?

First impressions of you and your business matter. You can say a lot with a business card, and because they supply content, they perform a necessary function within your content strategy. Never overlook the basics and always ensure your card has, at the very least:

- Your name
- Your role, aka what you do (if appropriate)

- The name of your business
- Your contact details, including email
- Your website address (URL)

And to be consistent with your brand, introduce:

- Your logo
- Your strapline

As a conversation starter and to fully exploit the opportunity to share content, you may want to include:

- Your social media engagement icons, for example, LinkedIn and Facebook
- A Quick Response, or QR, code for smart phones to scan and access website pages and therefore pages and promotions of your choice
- Hints and tips and other aide-memoire of your service
- Impactful images and graphics

To allow you to do this, you need to use not just the front but the back of the card and you can extend your capacity for delivering content further by a single-fold card doubling your space to make more of an impact.

You can also get really creative it you have the budget and use the size and format of a business card in many different ways, such as incorporating an integrated flash drive that holds your catalog or a "how to" guide on your products, more information on your business, or just a promotional gift. How about a business card–sized flower seed dispenser, breath mints, or, if you're a dentist, dental floss dispenser—you get the picture? Don't so much think "size"; think: What do I want to achieve with this? Today's digital print makes versioning of different cards for different teams, sectors, and markets easier and more cost-effective. The material you use to produce the card also has an impact on the receiver. A flimsy card with print that comes off on their fingers or rubs off on other stuff in their wallets or bags is shouting poor quality, as are spelling mistakes, mismatched fonts, and a poorly reproduced logo.

Today, smart, clear, and appealing business cards are not expensive and they often start your content conversation, so make them count.

CHAPTER 12

Successful Sales Copywriting Starts Here

So far we have looked at how to define your brand: who your core customers are, where you need to look to find them, and how you'll deliver content to them. We've looked at setting the tone and creating the right strapline to describe your business. We've also looked at the humble business card and how that begins the content conversation. Now we are going to look at different types of platforms and by this I mean different marketing collateral or Internet applications to deliver it. The ones you have identified as key to your customer will undoubtedly interest you most, but read up on the others too, to help ensure you have a wider picture of what potentially could help your business.

We have also touched on the fact that content marketing is not new; smart businesses have been doing it for a long time. The advent of new platforms simply gives us more ways to share and demands different approaches, but the basic requirement for high-quality content delivered through good copywriting remains the same. And keep in mind the central role of your content: to engage and promote.

For many years there has been an established and proven way to structure your copy in order to capture attention and sell more. This has especially been applied to direct marketing, where you identify, through lists or databases, your potential customers and send them marketing material designed to get an action or response: "buy now," "send for the brochure," "visit our website." The customers don't find you; you find them and ask for action.

Content marketing delivers engagement first and foremost. It helps customers find you, and, as such, they will be much more receptive to what you have to offer because they're already interested. But **don't throw the baby out with the bathwater**. Direct marketing copywriting techniques are tried, tested, and highly successful, so it makes sense to take what we know from them and apply that knowledge to the creation of content marketing copy.

> *Inspiration exists, but it has to find you working.*
> —Pablo Picasso

A painter who appeared to ignore all the rules of painting, Picasso knew his ability, and success at breaking those rules was based on the hard work of first thoroughly learning his craft.

What Are the Rules?

AIDA is the acronym developed in 1989 by E. St. Elmo Lewis to describe the stages a customer covers before making the decision to buy. It stands for:

- Attention
- Interest
- Desire
- Action

This formula remains the touchstone for adverts, direct mail, and all forms of promotional copywriting, both printed and online. Bringing us up to date, an additional element is added to the list after desire, and that is evidence or, as Andy Maslen puts it, conviction. Andy Maslen is a leading independent copywriter and his well-thumbed book *Write to Sell*[1] sits on my bookshelf. I recommend it highly.

As Andy explains, buyers today are bombarded by advertising and they become cynical. Conviction or evidence is the element that helps validate their decision to buy. In other words, it could be another customer's testimonial that will reassure them that the buying decision they are about to make is a sound one. Evidence can also take the form of "hard-data,"

---

[1] A. Maslen. 2009. *Write to Sell* (Singapore: Marshall Cavendish). ISBN 978-0-462-09975-0.

such as statistics, surveys, and polls—evidence that will convince a cynic. And so we now have AIDEA

- Attention—get it
- Interest—keep it
- Desire—create the need
- Evidence or conviction—justify the cost
- Action—tell them what to do next

There is also another system for ensuring you remember what needs to go into copy: the four P's:

- Promise—what's in it for the customer
- Picture—let them see themselves benefiting
- Proof—prove how valuable it is to them
- Push—ask for action from them

Here comes another in a "U" formation—*helpful for writing headlines:*

- Useful—focused on customer's needs
- Urgent—time specific
- Unique—compelling benefits
- Ultra-specific—say exactly what it is

Use whatever works for you to keep in mind the ultimate aim of the copy you are writing. Although the balance of emphasis will shift for content marketing to be "front-loaded" with less demand for action, remember we're giving, to get.

Why Use Them?

Whether you market your products and services B2B or B2C, AIDEA, the four P's, or all the U's offer useful reminders of basic selling principles within copywriting, a framework to touch base with when you approach content strategy and creation. Let's focus on AIDEA. What follows is a quick reminder guide:

Attention—It's All in the Headline

As many as five times the amount of people will read a headline than read the main body copy, so to capture interest in what you have to say, it really pays to get that headline right.

Benefits: Favorite by far are the headlines offering the reader a benefit to them: a warmer home, whiter teeth, greater savings, slimmer figure, faster car.

Free information: As with benefits, "How to" headlines that offer help and information are read and remembered more often—why pass up some good free advice?

News: Headlines attract eyes that include news and useful information worth passing on . . . etc. Your product may not be new but there may be a new way to use it.

Relevance: If you are looking for local clients and readers, put the name of your town/area in the title—people are far more interested in learning about the place they live than somewhere that is unlikely to have an impact on their lives.

Long or short? There's no hard and fast rule on this one. If it needs to be long, so be it. If it can be short, ditto—but try and keep it to one line.

Don't be too clever: Puns and double meanings will fail when you are competing for the attention of a busy person scanning a paper, newsletter, or website; you're likely to lose the interest of far more readers than you'll gain.

Flying blind: Similarly, try and avoid the temptation to write a headline that gives no clue to your content. These "blind" headlines don't perform well; again, who has the time?

Worst-case scenario? No headline at all.

Yeah, but hang on, how can someone see my headline when it's inside an envelope? Simple—put your headline on the outside of the envelope (there are two sides to every story and two sides to every envelope that I've ever seen).

Interest

Now you've got your reader's attention, you must capture their interest. Put yourself in their shoes, remember to employ empathy, and work out how what your offer applies to them. How it solves their problems, how it makes their lives easier? Talk about:

- **All the benefits**—what's in it for them, that is, what is valuable about your product? This is what they really want to know, backed up by
- **All the features**—facts, stats, and applications of your product
- **All the advantages**—the reasons why your product is right for them

For example, if I am looking for a digital alarm clock to buy, I'd be attracted by all the benefits of being awoken in the morning at the time of my choosing by hearing beautiful music from the obscure channel I love by a radio alarm clock that was simple to operate. The features to provide me with this experience would be three alarm settings, DAB digital tuning and sound quality, ergonomically designed and easy-to-use buttons (even when half asleep). The advantages of a state-of-the-art DAB digital radio is a dazzling array of stations to choose from and superior sound quality.

Desire

The game changer is "desire." Your customers are attracted and interested, but you have to change that emotion into real desire, a "must have," a "want." To do this, you play on (let's face it) their baser instincts:

- **Limit the supply**—they could lose out if they don't act quickly.
- **Create exclusivity**—they are only one of a few people selected.
- **Peer pressure**—get a head start on competitors, or mention others who are already benefiting.

- **Too good to miss**—"early-bird" offers of reduced price before a certain date.
- **Simplicity**—it's just so *easy* to do.
- **Exclusive expertise**—only you can offer them the service or product in the way they need it.

Evidence

Bombarded by marketing every day, more cynical or just more cautious, our customer needs more reasoned reinforcement to buy and this comes in the shape of evidence.

Evidence can take the form of any content that supports your claims. This could be a customer testimonial. Getting and using good testimonials is easier than you may think. A great promotional tool, we look at these in Chapter 20. Testimonials are an important part of your content marketing strategy and should figure throughout your content strategy.

Other evidence could be in the form of survey results, polls, and statistics. **This evidence needs to be truthful, accurate, and credited, or you stand a very real chance of damaging your brand.**

> *Lies, damned lies and statistics.*
> —Benjamin Disraeli

A famous example of an "interesting" set of statistics comes from cat food advertising. A well-known brand claimed that 8 out of 10 cats preferred their product. How so? Given that cats can't talk or understand the range of other food available, this statistic is as unlikely as it is daft. The reported statistic was then changed to 8 out of 10 owners who expressed a preference said their cats preferred it. Which is also pretty meaningless as "who expressed a preference" means that there are, in all likelihood, thousands of other owners and cats whose preferences are being ignored and unreported.

Honesty and accuracy is needed to build the kind of trust that will influence people's buying decisions. Using disingenuous or opaque statistics to inflate or disguise will, in the end, run counter to everything you are trying to build.

Action

You hope you have your customer convinced, so now you need to tell them what action to take next through **a call to action** (CTA). In direct marketing the key is to anticipate any barriers to your customer taking up your offer and eliminate them.

When someone wants something, they like to know exactly what to do, when, and how, so:

- Make it clear
- Make it simple
- Keep it short

At this point your customer doesn't want a lot of copy to wade through; they want to take action, so give them **all** the tools you can, including:

- Telephone number
- Email address
- Website with a buy-now button
- Uncomplicated order form
- Postal address

Direct marketing will usually use a command, such as "buy now." People may or may not follow your instruction, but at least they won't be in any doubt about what to do if they are keen.

Within content marketing the CTA is less stressed. Again, we're not direct selling, **but** it would be foolish not to offer ways to connect, share, find out more, comment and give feedback, sign up to receive more information, or visit a website. In other words, take an action that will not just inform them further but also begin and sustain engagement.

Let's move on and look at different ways you can deliver good, engaging content, both online and offline, and how to do it well and extend its impact by sharing it around.

CHAPTER 13

Brochures

Some traditional direct marketing tools can become more powerful when you integrate content marketing strategies. Helping to create and support greater engagement, the traditional sales brochure is one.

What Are They?

A printed brochure should be an enticing snapshot of the benefits your business brings; it can be about your top-selling products; it can focus on your expertise and history; it can be an instruction manual, *but* it cannot be all those things at once effectively. Whatever form your brochure takes, it should always be a powerful selling tool that is very clear in its objectives; it's also a great way to deliver engaging content.

- A brochure is a linear piece of marketing—there is a beginning, a middle, and an end.
- Its reach is limited.
- Its content is static and "locked" at the moment of creation.
- It is tactile—the look and feel creates a response from the recipient.
- It is highly disposable—once it's gone, it's gone.

Compared with a dynamic and interactive website, you may be led to believe that printed brochures are becoming redundant—not so, and the very fact that they are physical, linear, and static also gives them certain advantages, as we'll see. There is also a good crossover from digital to print by making your brochure downloadable from your website, offering your site visitors another way to get to know you better.

Why Use Them?

The very action of slowly licking a finger to turn a page of good-quality paper, the satisfying and reassuring "weight," shimmering images of streamlined brake discs, vibrant bedding plants, or this season's new line of tea dresses and accessories—what's not to love? Many people, myself included, still like to have something to leaf through on a break with a cup of coffee that doesn't involve powering up a screen.

A satisfying alternative to our smart phones, iPads, iPods, tablets, and flat screens, which when off means the content is out of sight and out of mind, a brochure cannot be turned off. The key to securing their place on a desk or tabletop, as with all content marketing, is to match your objectives to those of your core customer. Give them what they want, engage their interest, and you're well on the way to securing sales.

Boost the power and longevity of your brochure as a direct marketing tool by including greater content aimed at informing you customer, such as:

- A "how to" guide
- An article on your brand's history
- A pull-out-and-keep section of "top tips"
- A yearly planner
- Information on your work in the community
- Your contact details, address, website address, and logos of any social media you have a presence on, including, for example, Twitter, LinkedIn, Facebook, Instagram
- Testimonials from satisfied customers (see Chapter 20)

As a result your brand gains a stronger voice and your brochure gains greater value. Blending direct and content marketing techniques in this way furthers greater customer engagement and trust-building from the start of the relationship.

Think about Who You Want to Attract with Your Brochure

Your business will have a range of customers and new prospects that are at different stages of the buying process, for example:

- Some won't be aware of you at all.
- Some may be aware of your business and be generally interested.
- Some will have subscribed or signed up to receive more information.
- Some are on the point of purchase and need more in-depth technical detail.
- Some will already be knowledgeable customers and be happy to receive more information on innovation, product releases, or introductions to your partners and make referrals or invite friends and family to buy.

Having one brochure to please all these different types of customer isn't easy to pull off; one way or another you are likely to alienate or frustrate a proportion. It would, therefore, benefit you more to create three brochures for different stages of the buyers' process rather than one that is less likely to deliver the right content. Or you may decide to concentrate on one particular area, building up a series of over time, for example:

Brochure 1: New prospect with no knowledge of your business

Brochure 2: Subscriber/sign-up, enquiry into business or single purchase customer

Brochure 3: Regular customer that's open to new products and recommending you

Tailor your content to be of more value to the group you're focusing on, and **always base your literature not on what you know but on what your customers want to know**. Make it valuable to them, useful, and not simply a list of products; integrate your brochures into your content marketing strategy and they'll do a better job for your business.

Joining the dots: When putting together a great brochure, check:

- Successful copywriting starts here—Chapter 12
- How to write a headline—Chapter 14
- Testimonials—Chapter 20
- Spit 'n' polish—error-free zone—Chapter 21
- Ideas factory—Chapter 22

- A word on design—Chapter 25
- LET YOUR CONTENT DO ITS JOB—where can I SHARE?

Be careful about cutting and pasting wholesale from brochures, as it is specific to the job it's doing, but can you use the content in another form? For example, use the introduction and summary copy together with a downloadable version on your website.

CHAPTER 14

Press Releases and How to Write a Headline

Start your content conversation with a story . . .

What Are They?

A press release is not an advertisement; it is a way to attract attention by telling your business story and is a good way to raise your profile.

Why Use Them?

Press releases can show your resourcefulness, industry acumen, corporate social responsibility, and community involvement. All these will create interest in your business, reinforcing your credentials and attracting attention and potential new customers.

You can write and send out your own press release or use a PR agency to create and send them for you. Part of a PR agency's job is to forge good relationships with regional and national press. They may also specialize in niche industry publications or have expertise that will help you get your press release placed—but there are never any guarantees either for them or for you. Whether you choose to produce your own press releases or not, it is always worthwhile understanding how to put one together to attract press attention.

On any given day you will be competing with many other releases for an editor's attention amid daily news and the requirements of advertising. But they like and need local business news, so don't be put off, especially if you are reacting to current news or offer new information, such as survey results and new products.

How do you ensure your release is as "usable" as possible? In other words, how do you ensure that you give your release the best possible chance of publication? By making a journalist's or editor's job as easy as possible—they're busy people; they'll appreciate the help.

Here is my checklist for a well-crafted press release:

1. Strong headline: It needs to get attention, while giving a clear idea of content.

2. Who, what, where, when, and how: Miss out any of these elements and you will frustrate your reader. Try and get them into the lead paragraph.

3. Subsequent paragraphs should expand on the first paragraph and contain quotes.

4. Accuracy: If in doubt, don't use an unqualified piece of information or a quote—do your research properly, or it could be embarrassing.

5. Don't fall into the trap of using clichés or industry jargon—nothing turns people off quicker.

6. Don't waffle, 300 words to 600 words is a good length.

7. Ensure you remember all the relevant contact details and any notes to help editors on the background to the project/your organization. They will need these if they want to contact you for further information or undertake their own research.

8. Include an appropriate picture to accompany the press release. You'll stand a greater chance of being included in a publication if you have a great picture to illustrate what you're doing. Even if it is not used, it still plays a part in engaging the editor in the first place. And if you send the picture via email, which is highly likely, do make sure that the image is of a high enough resolution to print.

9. If you plan to submit your release online via an online press release service, such as PRWeb.com, they recommend you include a link to your business website within your lead paragraph. And later in your release copy, ensure you put in further links directly relating to your copy subject.

10. If you're sending out a press release yourself, it's worth getting the name of the relevant person at the publication, such as the business editor, and giving them a call to check they've received it and prompt them to read it.

11. Lastly, always bear in mind lead times; unlike newspapers, some magazines and publications are planned months in advance.

If you want your articles, press releases, and blogs to get read, then you need an attention-grabbing headline.

In Chapter 12, we looked at how to get "attention" and how as many as five times the amount of people will read a headline than read the main body copy, so to capture interest in what you have to say, it really pays to get it right. Here we'll recap what's needed to create a really good attention-grabbing headline.

First, don't feel you have to start your press release by writing the headline; more often than not, the headline can become a stumbling block when facing a blank screen or sheet of paper, so if nothing occurs to you straight away, simply put down a straightforward statement of what your press release is about and continue to write it. The right headline will occur to you as you craft your piece, and to help, as before, here is a reminder of my headline-writing tips:

Benefits: Favorite by far are the headlines offering the reader a benefit to them: a warmer home, whiter teeth, greater savings, slimmer figure, faster car.

Free information: As with benefits, "How to" headlines that offer help and information are read and remembered more often—why pass up some good free advice?

News: Headlines that include news—useful information and worth passing on. Your product may not be new but there may be a new way to use it.

Relevance: If you are looking for local clients and readers, put the name of your town/area in the title—people are far more interested in learning about the place they live than somewhere that is unlikely to have an impact on their lives.

Long or short? There's no hard and fast rule on this one. If it needs to be long, so be it; if it can be short, ditto, but try and keep it to one line.

Don't be too clever: For someone quickly scanning a paper, newsletter, or website, headlines with puns and double meanings don't get their attention. They don't have time and you're likely to lose the interest of far more readers than you'll gain.

Flying blind: Similarly, try and avoid the temptation to write a headline that gives no clue to your content; you'll be viewed as simply unhelpful.

Worst-case scenario? No headline at all.

Example of a press release

"BeeCause": York Creative Team Joins Yorkshire's Fastest Growing Environmental Scheme

The Big Ideas Collective (BIG) has recently signed up to Investors in the Environment (iiE) and, as part of their Silver Accreditation, have launched "BeeCause," an initiative to support a little creature that plays a big role in our health and environment: the honey bee.

BIG's Co-director Ned Hoste explained why the York-based creative marketing and publishing agency joined the iiE scheme: "We believe we all have a responsibility to look after what resources we have and particularly how, as a business, we can demonstrate our commitment and credentials. Investors in the Environment is a great way to do just that."

Committed to their local community and corporate social responsibility work, fellow Co-director Jacky Fitt explained why BIG has chosen to focus on the honey bee: "Industrious, highly social and collaborative, the honey bee has a great work ethic yet, sadly, it is under threat. One of nature's main pollinators, one out of every three mouthfuls of the food we eat arrives on our plate through pollination, so the fact that they are in decline is a real concern."

> With few wild bees left, the fate of the honey bee lies with the nation's beekeepers and through the British Beekeepers Association we have joined the 'adopt a beehive' scheme that enables us to support research into their welfare and protection.

The BIG plans to support a hive in every region of the UK, and to kick off this initiative they have already supported two hives, one in Yorkshire and a second in the northeast.

Further to the "BeeCause," earlier this year installation of solar panels now means their HQ is largely powered by the sun.

For more information about the BIG and their environmental achievements and to find out more about the honey bees, visit www .thebigideascollective.com.

Editor's notes:

Investors in the Environment
Contact: S. Omeone
Tel: 000 000 | Email: someone@iie.uk.com | Web: iie.uk.com

Investors in the Environment is a not-for-profit environmental accreditation scheme. It is designed to help the business sector save money and reduce their impact on the environment.

Big Ideas Collective Ltd
Contact: J. Fitt
Tel: 01904 270962 | Email: jacky@thebigideascollective.com
Web: thebigideascollective.com

The Big Ideas Collective is an innovative creative agency based in York, UK, working with clients throughout the UK and Europe on digital and print communication projects. Honorable Mention in the 2008 U.S. Green Dot Awards celebrating excellence in green products and services.

Image attached: L to R Ned Hoste and Jacky Fitt at local bee hives.

Remember

The capitalization of letters in a headline can sometimes trip people up. If you're feeling you're on bumpy ground, check Chapter 21, where you'll find my handy guide to title capitalization.

Joining the dots: When putting together a great press release, check:

- Successful copywriting starts here—Chapter 12
- Testimonials—Chapter 20

- Spit 'n' polish—error-free zone—Chapter 21
- Ideas factory—Chapter 22
- LET YOUR CONTENT DO ITS JOB—where can I SHARE?

Signpost to it from Twitter, LinkedIn, or a Facebook page. Post on your website or create a longer article for a blog.

CHAPTER 15

Newsletters

In Chapter 3, we touched on the history of content marketing. Remember *The Furrow* launched by U.S. agricultural machine manufacturers John Deere back in the late 1800s? And the original *Michelin Guide* that delivered maintenance and travel tips to motorists? From small beginnings, big profits flowed.

What Are They?

With so much marketing traffic moving online, the death of the printed newsletter has long been forecast, yet many examples continue to thrive. Why? Because that is the way a particular product's or service's customers like to receive their information. Remember, just because enthusiastic disciples of a new online platform claim instant and greater engagement, it doesn't mean that your customers are going to feel the same way immediately or in the near future. From your core customer profiling you should know how they like to receive their information, and if your customers like receiving their information in a regular printed newsletter, it's your job to make that newsletter as intriguing, valuable, and seductive as you can.

Why Use Them?

Without the interactivity of an email newsletter, giving the reader ways to access further information on a website or Facebook page, the printed newsletter, as with the printed brochure, is "linear." It has a beginning, middle bits, and an end. It is also highly tactile and its feel and weight produces a response from a recipient. Depending on what your business does—luxury high-end holidays or "stack-'em-high," "sell-'em-cheap" white goods—bear in mind you are conveying the quality and expectation of your brand through the quality of paper it's printed on and the way it's laid out, as well as the content within it.

With today's short-run digital printing costs, "versioning" and personalization of printed material has become more affordable. By adding your customer's name and altering the introduction to better reflect what you know about them, like the "Amazon approach"—"If you liked this, you might like this," etc.—they will feel like you are taking notice of them; you can make them feel special and they will be more interested in what you have to say.

So, how do you get the best from your printed newsletter?

1. **Timing**

   How often are you going to produce your newsletter? When would be the optimum time to send it out? This is going to depend on your sector and market and how much you have got to say. Are there any points in the year when your products sell at a premium, for example, firewood in early autumn, ice cream in warmer months, school bags just before the start of a new school term, and DIY products in good time for a bank holiday weekend? Using what you learned about your core customer in Chapter 3, you'll have a good idea of what . . . etc. If you are unsure, do more research. Speak to your current customers; watch your competitors and learn from them.

2. **Contents**

   Decide on the elements you are going to include. With the occasional variation, people like consistency and it's wise to set up a mix of your news, new innovations, case studies, team spotlight, community work, a guest column, season offers, etc. that will follow a regular pattern.

   Use the same techniques as with writing a press release (see Chapter 14) to craft headlines for articles and remember the who, what, where, when, and how of any piece or interview, to help ensure you cover all the main points.

   Remember, your printed newsletter is not about you—it's about your customer. Informative, exclusive, special, personal, the more you can focus your printed newsletters to your customers' needs, the better the response you will get. Tell them what they want to know and how you can make their lives easier or more profitable.

Use storytelling, ask questions, offer fresh ideas, and don't be afraid of a long, interesting copy.

Beware: humor (it may not be to everyone's taste), **"flowery" writing, and talking about yourself.**

What floats your particular boat is of no interest to them or their lives. And don't be afraid to ask for comment and feedback. From this you can better tailor your content and you'll be repaid with more repeat orders and referrals.

3. **Tone and style**

Think about the tone and style of your newsletter; your key audience needs to relate to it easily and feel comfortable reading it. **Make them feel special, intelligent, and loved.** Keep it "punchy"; don't waffle, and ensure it is accurate.

4. **Don't forget your CTA**

Give your customer plenty of ways to respond, give feedback, apply, buy, and come back to you for further information and advice.

5. **Layout**

Keep it clean: The main focus is a clear, easy-to-read, professional newsletter that reflects your brand. If you're including photographs, ensure they are of a good quality—not distorted or blurred. Work with a professional designer to create your template—it's a very worthwhile investment. If it looks amateurish, the journey from letterbox to recycling bin will be a swift one.

6. **Editing**

A newsletter may also present a challenge for smaller businesses, so delegate tasks and offer guest columns to associates and customers. But have one person as editor and arbiter of the "house style" and get a couple of people involved to help proofread. To help you with this, take a look at my proofreading guide in Chapter 21.

Publishing Schedule

To help ensure that you send your newsletter regularly, with the quality of content you want, put together a publishing diary or schedule.

Working with your printer and depending on how long they need to print, finish, and deliver your newsletter back to you, work backward from your desired posting date. Here's an example:

Three weeks before printer's deadline—decide on content topics

Seasonal articles

Check status of any new content available on your website

Upcoming events

PR

Offers

New commissions/testimonials *(don't forget to get sign-off from your customer)*

Start drafting and delegate work if needed—guest blog/team biography

One week before printer's deadline—Internal deadline for draft articles/intros/headlines

Edit and amend articles

Place copy and pictures/photos in designed template

Proofread

Deliver PDF to printer

Check printer's proofs

Proofread again

Receive printed newsletters and post out

Publication Day

Post PDF for download from your website

Send to your local press business or news desk/trade publications

And after . . .

Monitor how you're doing. Always check in with current and new customers if they have seen your newsletter and engage with them about it. Check with associates and partners to see if they will display and stock your newsletter. Think about which other outlets attract your key audience, and explore the possibility of them taking it.

Welcome feedback. You'll learn more from the negative than the positive feedback and this will help you build your audience and success.

Your most unhappy customers are your greatest source of learning.
—Bill Gates

Schedule follow-up calls if you have promoted new services or offers to prompt customer action.

Joining the dots: When putting together a great newsletter, check:

- Successful copywriting starts here—Chapter 12
- Press releases and how to write a headline—Chapter 14
- Testimonials—Chapter 20
- Spit 'n' polish—error-free zone—Chapter 21
- Ideas factory—Chapter 22
- A word on design—Chapter 25
- LET YOUR CONTENT DO ITS JOB—where can I SHARE?

Signpost to it from Twitter, LinkedIn, or a Facebook page. Post on your website or use articles as spring boards for blogs.

CHAPTER 16

Advertorials

What Are They?

An "advertorial" combines the words of an advert and an editorial. It is the name given to a piece of writing that replicates the editorial style of a printed or online newspaper or magazine—in terms of title, font style and size, picture formatting, and even column width. The piece is, however, paid for and the content provided by the featured business. These features will have "advertising promotion," "advertisement feature," "sponsored," or "sponsored feature" displayed at the top of the page or screen to make readers aware that they are really looking at a long-copy advert.

Most effective in combining news or human interest stories, the advertorial's popularity for businesses lies in the fact that, advert or not, people like to learn about stuff and are happy to read long copy if it's interesting, applies to their situation, and they feel they will benefit from it.

Why Use Them?

In what are called "split tests"—where the same product or service is promoted in different ways and the uptake measured—advertorials attract more readers and gain more recognition than short adverts nearly every time. This has been tested and proved many times over the years and continues to be true today. The advertorial offers businesses a way to get and keep readers' attention for longer, to really set out their stall, and, in terms of content marketing, pave the way to greater engagement by capturing a reader's interest and giving them valuable information. For example, recently I came across two advertorials.

The first was for a well-known brand of battery. A full-page, full-color feature, it was not, however, immediately obvious it was anything to do with batteries. The feature was focused on cameras and explored the best cameras for family use: something smart and clever for dad and mum and, more robust, easier to use for the kids. The feature had plenty of happy family pictures of everyone snapping away, a brief "how to" guide to help improve your photography, and a short review of a range of cameras. All very helpful if you like or are thinking of buying a camera. What the feature also did was remind readers that you need a good, long-lasting battery to power the cameras and keep everyone happy—and you want to keep everyone happy, right? When readers think about powering up their cameras, they'll be reaching for the "right" battery to help.

The second feature was for toothpaste. The main focus of this advertorial, again a full-page color feature, was pregnancy and how to keep healthy. Of great interest not just-to-mums to be, but also family and friends, the advertorial focused on well-being and how to pamper yourself, including a competition to win a spa break. Stats about gum disease problems in pregnancy were underlined by expert opinion from the clinical director of a dental practice. Again, branding was discreet, far outweighed by pictures of healthy, smiling pregnant women, all of whom were undoubtedly confident in the health of their teeth and gums while coping with everything else pregnancy has in store. It's just one less thing to worry about, so why not get the right toothpaste from a company that clearly cares?

Putting Together Your Advertorial

What Are You Selling?

Even though you are preparing content from the point of view of addressing your customer's pain, soothing their fears, or informing them, the first thing to do before writing an advertorial is to define very clearly in your mind what it is you are selling. When you know this, it is much easier to find a story that's going to be a good vehicle and help deliver the right messages. If, for example, you have an accountancy company, do you want to sell the full range of your services, your bookkeeping service for sole traders, or just your tax services to SMEs? Get specific, it will help.

What's the Story?

Remember what your core customer will be looking for—create a good title that will get their interest and craft copy that will keep it, using:

- Value—informative, opinion-changing, useful: *how to guides, top tips, expert advice*
- Currency—newsworthy, trending, influencing: *polls, stats, innovation*
- Story—inspiration, vision, ideas, journey: *personal, adversity, success*
- Emotion—desire, joy, fear, relief, envy: *get more, be better, win a, beware of*

Set the Style

Make sure you check the style and tone of the magazine or paper in which you are going to place your advertorial and the requirements of their advertorial policy. Check out your competition. Bearing in mind your brand tone and style, ensure that you are writing in a natural way to appeal to that particular readership. Steer clear of any strong CTAs, your strapline, or anything else that might kill the mood—you're giving to get.

Story, Not Sales

Any mention of a product or services should be kept to the middle section of the feature. Include statistics to illustrate and validate what you are saying if you can.

He Said, She Said, They Said . . .

Quote expert third parties if you are talking about statistics and especially to portray benefits. These read as customer testimonials and are great sales messages in themselves.

Use Photography Wisely

Illustrate your story, *not* your product, and use captions.

Forget about the Price Tag

Don't include any prices for products and services, but do make sure that if the reader wants to get in touch, they can do so easily by putting in your contact details, including any social media platforms you can be found on.

Bait the Hook

Consider including a competition prize if this is within your budget. But, again, don't make it about the product you're selling, make it about the story you're telling.

Byline

By using a "byline," in other words naming the author of your feature, you will give the piece greater credibility and also promote the idea that it was written specifically for the publication and reader.

Sit It within Your Marketing Strategy

Check back with your overall strategy and the different channels you are using to reach your core customer. Plan your advertorial and talk about it through your website and social media. Promote it to your associates and think also of ensuring a consistent approach—three or four advertorials regularly released in a printed or online publication over 6 months will be more effective than one or two and then nothing. If it forms part of a series, signpost the next installment if appropriate. Welcome feedback and monitor results.

Joining the dots: When putting together a great advertorial, check:

- Successful copywriting starts here—Chapter 12
- Press releases and how to write a headline—Chapter 14
- Testimonials—Chapter 20
- Spit 'n' polish—error-free zone—Chapter 21
- Ideas factory—Chapter 22
- LET YOUR CONTENT DO ITS JOB—where can I SHARE?

  Signpost to it from Twitter, LinkedIn, or a Facebook page. Post on your website and carry on "the story" online.

CHAPTER 17

Emails and Email Marketing

Emails are one of the most effective ways to deliver your content. Used for direct marketing, yes, but more effectively used within your content marketing strategy to keep your customers up to date with your services and reach out to new prospects. It's quite possible that in some instances email may be the only written communication your customer receives from you. If this is the case and even if it isn't, it pays to get the content of your emails working hard for you and engaging your readers above and beyond the day-to-day project-related traffic.

This is the age of electric ink.

—Robert McCrum

What Are They?

Email marketing is the sending of emails to raise awareness about your products and services, present an offer, and invite engagement. A big advantage of email marketing is that you can target and track responses accurately and, therefore, measure your return on investment more precisely. Many people like and want to receive information on products and services that they are interested in, in order to help them make better buying decisions.

Email marketing can be a very worthwhile element of your content marketing strategy, but beware, you are required by law to get permission, consent, or "opt in" from your customers and prospects before they receive your email marketing. Firing out unsolicited marketing emails is illegal and is known as spam or spamming.

It is you responsibility to know the law and how to apply it to your business; there are stiff penalties for those who don't. Do your research and check with a legal specialist.

To help businesses curate email database lists, create campaigns, and collate responses, there is a range of free and paid-for software tools, including MailChimp® and Constant Contact®, together with bespoke systems that web developers build to work seamlessly with their clients' websites.

Why Use Them?

The digital workhorse, emails deliver content around the globe every minute of every day and remain a great way to inform, promote, and engage with your core customer and interested new prospects.

Best Footer Forward

Possibly because of its now mundane, everyday use, email communication can often be overlooked as a great "drip" content marketing tool. What do I mean?

Every email **you send gives you the opportunity to share content and should be considered as part of your content marketing strategy.**

Simply through short messages within your email "footer," you have the opportunity to alert customers to the availability of new content like blogs, articles, and guides. Let's start at the beginning and look at your email footer, also known as your sign-off, signature, or boilerplate.

Do you even have one? You should, and not just because it looks professional. Depending on where you are based and if your business is registered/incorporated, there are legal regulations that cover what information you must give people as part of your business communication. **It is your responsibility to ensure you know what is required, how it applies to you, and how you can follow it in your region/state and country.**

Further to this and importantly, your industry may require you to make specific disclosure statements, for example, if you work in the legal, financial, or health profession. Businesses may also include a disclaimer that limits their liability if the email contains confidential material and gets sent to the wrong person in error or, inadvertently, is the route through which a virus gets into a computer. I would highly recommend checking with a legal specialist about any and all legally required business communication content.

By adding your logo and strapline, you ensure a joined-up, consistent approach to your branding across all your communication and content, making your business more memorable (and it looks more professional).

By including your website and social media links, you are offering your recipients other ways to connect and learn about you.

You can set up a "default" email footer through an email "signature" feature of your email software, via a firewall, an antivirus, or an antispam system or by the server that handles your messages.

The key is to make your sign-off clear, professional, and straightforward with all the content the recipient may need, including embedded links to your website, your social media accounts, and routes to additional, valuable content. The font can also be smaller than the main body text and this often looks better. But don't make it too small; it is there to be read.

Bob is a builder. As an example, here's Bob's email footer:

Kind regards,
Bob Brown
CEO
Brown's Builders *"For a greater understanding"*
Brown's Builders Inc. 1 Brick Street, San Francisco. CA 94100
Phone: 1 200 345 6789 | 708 222 4567
bob@browns.com | www.browns.com | Instagram
This email and any attachment(s) is confidential and for the addressee only. If sent in error please notify the sender and/call 1 200 345 6789 and delete it. All content is © Brown's Builders Inc. Brown's Builders accept no responsibility for loss or damage howsoever arising from the email's use, including from a virus.

Bob decided not to include his logo or any images because he wanted to ensure that his footer would appear correctly on his customers' many different email systems, but he can use his logo/brand colors to highlight the business name and strapline. If you do choose to use your logo, ensure your email footer is tested on all the email systems you can. If recipients have, for some reason, set their privacy permissions to block pictures, the logo will just look like an empty little box and, sadly, there is nothing you can do about that.

What to avoid?

- Don't use too many different-sized fonts, too many bold colors, and capitalized words. This just makes your footer look amateurish at best, alarming at worst, and capitalized words read like you are SHOUTING.
- Don't cut and paste in adverts that clearly haven't been designed for the footer, apart from the fact that any pictures or logos may not download correctly or may be blocked on your customer's email system; it often has the same effect as the first point.
- Don't frustrate your customer with broken links. If you have links in your email footer, make a habit of testing them regularly.
- Don't get too complicated. A footer that may look great in your software may look poor on another web-based email system and logos may not translate well. For this reason it is worth getting your web developers to check the footer and TEST IT (yes, I'm shouting) across all the main email systems before you begin using it.

Marketing Emails

Further to your day-to-day emails and the footer that is going to quietly do its marketing job for you, let's look at more specific campaigns directed at your "opt-in" recipients. I mentioned earlier free and paid-for software tools such as MailChimp and Constant Contact that help you create and curate your campaigns and these are well worth using.

Saving you time and effort, these tools have been developed specifically to make the business of distributing content a "no brainer," making the delivery to your customers and prospects as professional and straightforward as possible. In brief you can:

- Import your email lists
- Create a professional template with your own logo, or choose to design your own

- Track your results closely, and thus measure your return on investment easily
- Integrate them with analytics on your website to track clicks and other applications such as event booking
- Segment your lists, enabling you to refine your targeting
- Test different content with different segments—to see what content works best
- Link them with your social media platforms, including Twitter and Facebook.

A professional, well-written, branded, and regular email delivery, offering valuable content delivered straight to your customer's and opting-in prospect's inboxes, is a great way to get your content read and shared. Many have predicted the demise of email marketing, but not so. It may be seen by some as "old hat" but its more-focused reach often proves highly successful.

Don't be the business that decides to place their content inside an attached PDF. My heart always sinks when I receive one of these—it makes me think of the missed opportunities for the sender. Who knows what's inside the boring little PDF icon? I don't and I'm busy and on to the next item in my inbox so I'll never know. The free tools on offer for your email marketing give your emails immediate impact, so use them. Anything else nowadays is pretty inexcusable.

Let's have a look at how to set up and run your email content marketing campaign. A quick tip before we get going. Get on the lists to receive your competitors' email marketing to discover how and when they do it and what content they deliver. All of this will inform and inspire your own ideas and help ensure that your content is better than theirs.

Setting Up Your Email Content Marketing

1. **Work out what you want to achieve**
   As with any element of your marketing tool kit, be clear on what outcomes you want to achieve and measure your success against these. For example, four new business clients over the next 6 months or an increase in turnover of 3 percent. Be realistic and remember that you

are building trust and consistency through quality content—this is a long-term strategy not a "smash and grab."

2. **Segment your list**

   Direct emails give you the opportunity to split up or segment your database and allow you to send different messages to different segments of your market, tailored to interest them most. If you are, say, a florist, you will have different market segments including, for example, businesses, hotels, weddings, and the general public.

3. **Decide what you're going to say**

   No doubt this element will be part of your discussions around when to send your emails out. How much content you need or want will impact on how often you can send them, yet they don't want to be overly long. With this in mind it helps to create a list of topics from which you can choose, depending on what is happening/is most appropriate. For example:

   • Portfolio update
   • Latest news
   • Seasonal offer
   • Team members
   • Blog
   • Events
   • Testimonial
   • "How to" guide

   Writing reams is not necessary and will be hard to sustain, so just pick four or five topics every time.

   Your customer is the most important person, so make the content all about them.

   Remember: Check in with your goals for the content via AIDEA (see Chapter 12); don't follow it slavishly but be aware of crafting your content with your outcomes in mind.

   Your reader wants to know how your products and services can benefit them. Remember how everyone likes to feel special, intelligent, and loved? Use your direct emails to promote valuable information that makes them feel special, gives them insider knowledge, and shows you care and they'll be delighted. Make sure you suggest they share the content to associates and colleagues and they just might.

4. **Ensure you give your marketing email a good subject line**

   When your email lands in your customer's or prospect's inbox, it will only show the subject line. If you want them to open it, it had better be enticing. Again, put yourself in your customer's shoes. What would make you open an email from a business, especially when you are busy? Your aim is to make your readers feel straightaway that they will learn or benefit by the click . . .

   For example:
   Business howlers and how to avoid them
   Ten ways to grow prize-winning tomatoes
   How to write error-free copy every time—you get the picture?

   Undertaking a series of A/B split tests—an analysis of 1,720 campaigns, sent to 6,226,331 inboxes, MailChimp discovered that using your business name early within the subject line, more often than not, attracted better results. Telling your recipients who an email is from gives them more confidence to open it.

   Avoid words that may land you in people's "junk" file. Most email servers are actively filtering out emails with potentially "spammy" words in subject lines, including free, stock, eBay, password, mortgage, etc. These can trigger spam detection software, so keep them out of your subject line.

   As well as avoiding dodgy words, don't use an exclamation mark. Similar to using capital letters, it comes across as overenthusiastic and like shouting. Be confident, be creative, but don't shout at your customer; it's off-putting.

5. **Write your content**

   Remember that your reader will be scanning your content quickly, so keep your copy concise. Create strong headlines and front-load your newsletter items with the important information in the first lines, as you would with a press release (see Chapter 14). People will often just read the first few lines of an article before moving on to the next item.

   Use front-loaded introductions and link to a longer article or blog on your website if you have one (you should have one, more on that a little later). Once on your website you have all the other tools to offer expanded content, track your visitors, capture their data, plus introduce them to new and different content they may be interested in.

Good, interesting, and inspiring ideas are literally walking and talking all around us. When it comes to inspiration for ideas, if you're feeling a little stuck, take a look at Chapter 22 for some food for thought.

Use the same tone and style that you use in other elements of your content marketing. Part and parcel of your brand behavior: fun and informal, or friendly professional, replicating your tone and style also reassures your reader that your brand really knows what it's about and is delivering a consistency of quality content across everything you do.

6. **Don't forget your CTAs**

When you have drafted and proofed your email, don't forget your CTA—what you would like your reader to do. When you have captured your customer's attention and they have digested some, if not all, of your content, help them out by telling them what you would like them to do or offer them options. We are not direct marketing, but it's reassuring for people to know what they need to do simply and clearly should they want to learn more or get in touch. The worst thing you can do is waste their time by making them guess, or offer no way for them to contact you.

7. **Encourage them to share your content**

Importantly, ensure you allow your recipients to share your content, view an online web version (as opposed to opening the template on their PC or Mac) and unsubscribe or "opt out" if they wish to. This is important for professionally run email marketing campaigns and is a legal requirement in many countries now. If you are using a free or fee-paying template, these should be automatically added for you.

8. **Add links and make sure they work**

Try to avoid using links from words within the body of your copy or "inline" links. This will take the reader's attention off what you are saying and they may click out of your newsletter before an important bit. Place your links at the end of an article and clearly label them, so that your reader knows the source. Accurate, authentic, and appropriate links and resources are also part and parcel of good practice and brand behavior.

9. **Decide when you are going to send your emails**

   It's important to plan and diary the preparation and sending out of your emails. With busy schedules to keep up and unexpected events, it's all too easy to forget to leave enough time to create and collate quality copy. Don't forget, this a really important element of content marketing, which will promote sharing and increase conversions. Once a month, once every 2 months—decide what is realistic and doable and stick to it. In this way you will build trust and consistency for your brand. Too often businesses manage the first three emails, then there is a big gap, until one emerges some time later. Plan them so that it is manageable for you and your team and make that plan over a period of 6 months to a year with review points to highlight any issues or particular challenges.

10. **Have a "zero tolerance" approach to errors**

    For all content you send out, do your utmost to ensure it is error free. There is nothing more unprofessional than mistakes, typos, and spelling errors in copy. See Chapter 21 on proofreading for some great strategies and tools to avoid publishing errors.

11. **Create a publishing diary or schedule**

    To help ensure that you send your emails regularly, with the quality of content you want, put together a publishing diary. Work backward from your desired publishing date, for example, every third Thursday of the month, and track what you will need when and from whom. Adjust the timings to suit the way you work. For example:

One week before publication—*decide on content topics*

   Check the status of any new content available on website

   Upcoming events

   PR

   Offers

   New commissions/testimonials *(don't forget to get sign-off from your customer)*

   Start drafting and delegate work if needed—guest blog/team biography

Two days before publication—*deadline for draft articles/intros/headlines*
Edit and amend articles
Load up onto marketing email template/software
Proofread including testing all web links
Test—send it to yourself and one or two others on different browsers, for example, Google Chrome, Firefox, Safari, Opera, Microsoft Edge, etc. Get feedback on how it looks; do all the links work?

One day before publication
Final amends
Proofread again
Schedule publication

Publication day
Proofread again
Send or check email has been sent out
Promote on any social media—Twitter, Facebook, Google+, etc.

And after . . .

Monitor how you're doing *and what content is the most popular.*
- **Who opened the email?**
- **Which articles gained clicks to further information?**
- **Who has responded to content by getting in touch?**
- **Check on any "hard bounces" that mean any emails that failed to reach their destination—is the email address incorrect or has the person left that position? This will help you keep your data clean and more effective for future campaigns.**
- **Are you stimulating the kind of interest/sales you want?**

Test to Improve

It's also worth doing some testing on your email newsletters to improve the uptake. You can do this by randomly segmenting your database—most simply into an A group and a B group (also known as AB Testing). Test responses to your email by:

- **Developing two different subject lines**
- **Sending out at two different times of the day or days of the week.**
- **Craft two different CTAs.**
- **Again, using free commercial software, this is straightforward to do and you can easily monitor which newsletter delivers the greatest number of opens and clicks to your website, which will help you refine future newsletters.**

Joining the dots: When putting together a great marketing email, check:

- Successful copywriting starts here—Chapter 12
- Press releases and how to write a headline—Chapter 14
- Testimonials—Chapter 20
- Spit 'n' polish—error-free zone—Chapter 21
- Ideas factory—Chapter 22
- A word on design—Chapter 25
- LET YOUR CONTENT DO ITS JOB—where can I SHARE?

Signpost to it from Twitter, LinkedIn, or a Facebook page. Send to business and news desks; post on your website in a newsletter archive section.

CHAPTER 18

Websites

In the next chapters, we'll look at the factors that create good online content.

No matter what you do or how big your business, when people have heard about you or met you, want to find your services, and check you out, they will go online and look at your website—**FACT**. *If you're in any doubt about this, along with climate change deniers, you are in a vanishing minority. If you don't want your customers to find you and learn more about your business easily, by all means don't have one.*

Your Online Content Hub

Your website is your shop window for the world and a powerful marketing tool. It is crucial to get the content for your website right to ensure you give your site visitors and the search engine spiders that help rank your site the best possible experience.

Together with explaining what you do, how, and why, get your content marketing hat on and look at your website copy from the point of view of why a customer would want to **buy from you, contact you,** and, importantly, **come back for more.**

If you are tempted to simply copy across the words currently used in your brochure onto your website, don't. There are some very important reasons why you'll be letting your business down and missing lots of content marketing opportunities.

- A brochure is a linear piece of marketing: There is a beginning, a middle, and an end.
- Its reach is limited.

- Its content is static and "locked" at the moment of creation.
- Its highly disposable; once it's gone, it's gone.

Whereas

- A well-designed and coded website is dynamic, offering the visitors different ways to find the information they want.
- It has global reach.
- It has the ability to show different visitors different content.
- Content can be updated and amended as often as desired.
- Social media and "live chat" offer real-time engagement.
- Search engine optimization techniques give the owner the ability to make it more "visible"—pushing it up the organic[1] search engine listings.
- Tracking software like Google Analytics gives site owners statistics on the site's effectiveness—what content is popular and what is not attracting their attention.

Brochures and leaflets will always have a role in the marketing tool kit and play a part in content marketing; however, a website is a completely different creature. Although your "tone of voice" and key messages should be consistent across all your marketing, your approach to writing content for your website needs to take account of the platform and workings of the Internet as well.

Every day your brand is being judged. Quickly comparable to those of your competitors, visitors to your website are assessing your professionalism, expertise, value to them, and ability to deliver.

When someone sits at their computer screen and views a website, they begin a direct "conversation" with that site. If the site doesn't speak to them in a language they understand, or can relate to easily, it's just a mouse click back to the search engine listings and your competitor's site.

------

[1] An "organic" search engine ranking is the listing of a website that is ranked on the relevancy of its content to the search words used, as opposed to a paid-for listing, which may or may not.

Using the key messages and establishing your chosen tone of voice, the content on your website needs to quickly and simply reassure your visitors that they have reached the right place and lead them into the site to find out more.

Brand and Tone

Your core values, actions, and messages all come into play to engage your site visitors. You need to reassure them they are in the right place, getting information and advice from the right people. As discussed earlier, the tone and style of how you present your content play a very important role in how you are perceived and understood.

Remember, your copy should speak directly to your visitors by using the first person and second person form, for example, we, us, and our; you and your, consistently across the whole website.

Your tone should be welcoming, reassuring, and knowledgeable and not overly formal. More conversational than a brochure, a website gives you the opportunity to begin a direct relationship with a customer. It shows them that you are not just highly experienced but very approachable, dependable, and responsive to their needs.

The design or visual look of your website is also fundamental to the professionalism of your brand. Although we are concentrating on the creation and delivery of copy, Chapter 25 of this book is a short, yet important chapter on design. Please don't skip it. It will save you time and money and also save you from looking like you don't value your own brand.

Writing for the Web

As it stands when writing this book, when you write a website, you are writing for a human **and** a robot. The human is of course your customer or web visitor. The robot is a web crawler or "spider." These are all names given to an automated program that systematically roams the Internet indexing page content in order to list and rank websites for search engines.

Your site visitors are your customers. Without them you won't have a business.

The search engine spiders rank your site. Without them your site won't get many visitors, if any.

Both are very important, but without doubt the human visitor is your primary concern, because people buy products and services, not search engines. Your content will inform your visitor, and from the moment they land on your page, it's the beginning of your relationship with them.

You know when you are reading a good website. It's a compelling combination of the informative, persuasive, knowledgeable, and relevant, always with benefits for visitors upfront and infused with the personality of the brand through its "tone of voice."

Content Management Systems

Time was when sites were built without content management systems (CMS). This meant that as a site owner, you had to contact your busy web developer if you wanted to alter any text, add a page, or change a picture, all deeply frustrating, costly, and inevitably slow. Happily, today the vast majority of sites come complete with their own CMS. This may be bespoke, or be more standardized for template sites. This is fundamental to you as the website owner—*always* have control of the content on your site.

CMS gives you lots of flexibility to change elements of your site, predominantly copy and graphics, blogs, news articles, events calendars, galleries, etc. and put in place good search engine optimization (SEO) practices.

The following are some key guidelines for crafting website copy content, which will help give both your visitors and the search engine spiders what they are looking for. I will expand further on SEO a little later on.

Engaging, readable, and natural copy is your goal because ultimately people buy products, services, and ideas, not search engines.

First let's look at writing for the most important person: your website visitor.

When sitting down to write or rewrite website content, it can be difficult to get started, so here's a good strategy that will deliver results:

1. You know your subject; don't think too hard about it; simply "brain dump" your ideas for your content. Don't worry about format or different pages at this stage.

2. Now make a note of all the benefits to your clients from using your services. If, say, you are a solicitor, you may want to highlight:
   - Protection
   - Problem solving
   - Reducing risk
   - Peace of mind

   Take what you know from identifying/establishing that core customer we looked at earlier, together with your core values and actions. Also, ask yourself: "What is the question that prompts the answer: 'To buy from my business'?" This will help ensure you are teasing out all the benefits.

3. Jot down your key words and phrases; again, taking the example of a solicitor, it may well be divorce proceedings, litigation, commercial dispute, conveyancing. These are the terms that people will type into a browser like Google or Bing to search for your services.

   Your **key words and phrases** are often identified in conjunction with your web developer or professional copywriter who can advise, through research, the best and most appropriate ones to use for your business and services. You'll also find online software tools to do this yourself, including the useful free tool Google AdWords. We will look at these key words in greater depth in the next section about SEO. As you write, you must keep these in mind and use them where you can in **a relevant and natural way**. A good rule of thumb is a key word density of 4 to 5 percent of your page copy word count. Use them within your headlines and early on in your introductory text.

Things that brains like:

- Alliteration—think: intelligence, impact, and inspiration
- The rule of three—see above and how comfortable it feels to read
- Personality—like people, if it's missing, time drags
- Short sentences—makes stuff easy to read and digest

- Good punctuation—see above
- Around 250 to 350 viewable words on the page—get to the point
- CTAs—tell people what you would like them to do; they prefer it

4. When you have outlined what content you want to share, think about splitting it across different pages for your site. As well as the usual "about us" and "contact us" pages, split your pages into subject information that your core customer would want to find.

5. Within your pages, shape your introductory paragraph to always include:
   - Benefits
   - Key words

6. Within the following paragraphs go on to explain how you work and why you are effective. Keep bearing in mind your key words and introduce them in subheadings to help break up the text for readers. Use bullet points where appropriate.

7. Watch out for repetition. Use synonyms—words that largely mean the same thing—to help avoid this. For example, fast, swift, prompt, timely. See Chapter 21 for some help here.

8. Always set out any acronyms in full first, for example, non-governmental organization (NGO), after which, if you mention them again, you can simply use the initials. Although some are very much part of our common understanding, for example, LED (light-emitting diode); many of us choose not to offer the full version of very well-known acronyms, including NASA, NATO, PhD, RSVP, SCUBA, and YMCA. Just bear in mind that if a visitor to your site doesn't understand your acronyms or industry jargon, they will feel alienated and will show this by simply clicking off your site and looking elsewhere. If in any doubt, put it in full first.

9. Insert short quotes or "pull quotes" from longer client testimonials. These are a great way to break up sections of text and reinforce your message of benefits to site visitors.

10. Can you cross-sell any services or products? Bear in mind how one piece of information can lead onto another. Use the power of your website by offering different ways to reach relevant information. *Think* how your services or products complement one another, and use the "if you like this, you may also like this . . ." approach—a favorite with the hugely successful online retailer Amazon.

11. Don't forget your CTA. Clear and informative works best—in creating the desire in your visitor to contact you, tell them what you would like them to do. For example, "Please get in touch to . . ." or "Buy now to receive your discount . . ."

12. Go back over your piece and cut down the word count to make it as concise and relevant as possible. A total of 250 to 350 words is a good guide for main pages. Other pages will differ as appropriate, but don't expect people to endlessly scroll down. This is especially true now as more and more of us are searching on our smart phones and tablets. There are also good tools around to help you work out how easy your copy is to read. These readability indexes include the Flesch-Kincaid Index and the Gunning Fog Index, to name just two. They give you a U.S. grade level required to read the copy. A good rule of thumb is to aim for a grade level of around seven. This represents a reading age of around 12 years in the UK and, therefore, largely accessible to all. I am discussing generalities here; for highly academic or complex products and procedures, this, of course, won't necessarily apply. Flesch Reading Ease statistics are also very useful and so popular that you'll find them within word-processing packages including Microsoft Word. A score of reading ease of around 60 tells you that the text will be generally understandable by 13 to 15-year-olds. The higher the score on this scale, the easier it is to read.

13. Finally, get someone else to read, comment, and proof your copy for typos and errors. Sometimes when you are very close to what you do, you can miss the blindingly obvious! For help, check our proofreading tips in Chapter 21.

In beginning our online relationship with our clients, informative, interesting, and well-written copy means they are better prepared to talk to us; we can manage their expectations and keep developing our website to meet their needs.

Legal bit—If you seek to capture your website visitors' data through your site, in other words their email address, payment details, and any contact details, you need to be aware of and adhere to your regional/state and country legal requirements regarding data protection. Similarly, if you operate within a regulated profession and/or operate an e-commerce site (you are an online seller), again, you need to be aware of and compliant with current data protection, and the content of your website must reflect this. These may include a Terms and Conditions of Usage Policy, a Privacy Policy, a "Cookie" alert,[2] and an SSL certificate to ensure any personal data delivered via your website is encrypted for security.

Particularly e-commerce and more general websites should also have a secure sockets layer, or SSL certificate to ensure that any data passed to a business via its website is secure and protected from attack. In late 2017 Google's popular browser Chrome introduced a visual ident for letting web browsers know which sites were, or were not, protected with SSL certificates. I can only imagine the rest will follow suite. If you don't already have one, I recommend talking to your website developer about an SSL certificate for your website. **All good web developers should be aware of current regulation and legal requirements, but this is no defense, and as the business owner you must make sure you know what your duties and responsibilities are.**

Joining the dots: When putting together a great website, check:

- Successful copywriting starts here—Chapter 12
- Press releases and how to write a headline—Chapter 14
- Testimonials—Chapter 20
- Spit 'n' polish—error-free zone—Chapter 21
- "Que?"—lost in translation—Chapter 23
- A word on design—Chapter 25
- LET YOUR CONTENT DO ITS JOB—where can I SHARE?

Signpost new content to your followers every time it is updated from Twitter, LinkedIn, Google+, or your Facebook page. Could a new article, product, or project make a good press release or be the basis for a new "how to" guide?

---

[2]Cookies are small bits of text that are embedded within websites to help them perform better and give the site visitor a better experience. Depending on how your website is developed, you will have some form of cookie in there and they work by identifying the website visitor from their IP address. It is a legal requirement in many regions/states and countries to alert your website visitor that there are cookies on your website and give them a way to "opt out" of being identified by them.

Search Engine Optimization

SEO is the art of getting noticed for what you do by search engine spiders.

For the best results, well-written, quality content needs to go hand-in-hand with good SEO.

Search is the main driver to content.
—Outbrain

The engaging way in which a copy on effective, content-rich websites is written, together with sound SEO techniques, will raise your website's profile, thus attracting more visitors, and will push it up the search engine rankings. So, it is well worth understanding a little more about what goes into good SEO.

Content is the reason search began in the first place.
—Lee Odden, TopRank Marketing

Your website CMS should give you access to curating your SEO. Template sites such as Word Press offer "plugins" like Yoast for straight-forward SEO input.

70% of links searchers click on are organic.
—SearchEngineJournal.com

As discussed in the previous section, identifying your key words and phrases is crucial, as this is the currency of search engine spiders. These spiders, as we'll see, check the use of key words in website addresses, in titles, and in headings as well as the amount of key words on the page (key word density) to offer searchers the most relevant sites. You can help yourself by working out the best key words to use on your website by using online key word software. Start with the free elements of Google AdWords. Plenty of established fee-paying software are also available. Your choice depends on what is appropriate for your business, so do a little research before you buy.

Let's look at the current, most important elements of what goes into good SEO.

First and foremost a well-designed, well-coded, and accessible site is *always* going to be more visible to search engines, and thus searchers, than a poorly designed and badly developed one. Your website is your shop window for the world, underlining the quality of your brand, product, and services and the hub for all your online content; *resist* the urge to cut corners.

What's Vital?

Quality content: Relevant, well written, and, most importantly, unique. This is what people and search engines are both looking for. If you have cut and pasted other people's words into your website, beware; that's copyright infringement and, apart from the search engine spiders steering clear, it's an illegal practice.

New content: How often you update your website with unique, quality content matters. If your website remains unchanged for a long time, people won't return and neither will the spiders, which will damage your search engine rankings.

Key words in your URL or web address: For each page of your website, have the relevant key words in the URL; for example, if your business is called Bath Time Bubbles and you produce a line of plastic ducks, it would be worth having www.bathtimebubbles.com/plastic-ducks for your page specifically promoting plastic ducks.

Key words in your page title: <title tag>: six to eight words (65 characters), with your key word near the start. The words you use here will show up as the title of your page in the search results.

Key words in your web copy headings and subheadings: Ensure that the words figure in your body text too, which helps with the following.

Key word density: Make sure that you have your main key words in your text, but don't shoe horn them in unnaturally. This is known as key word stuffing and can actually harm your site ranking.

High-quality inbound links (also known as backlinks): Inbound links or backlinks are those links **to** your site **from** other websites. It is really helpful to have links to your site from other high-traffic, highly reputable websites. Links from national organizations or membership bodies spring to mind, also expert associates within your sector, including project partners. They help authenticate your site and your content. Check with your website developer that any backlinks, if clicked on, open in a new window or tab. This means that your site visitor, although checking out or validating you via your inbound links, will come back to your main site once they close the inbound link window. *Have as many backlinks as you like; just **watch the quality**, that's what counts.*

Key words in inbound anchor text: Anchor text describes a link **within** the text on a web page. Your ranking will be improved if you have your key words within inbound anchor text links from a third-party site, which will take visitors to a page on your website. For example, On a reputable associate's website page you might have "Enjoy non-toxic plastic ducks for bath time fun!" The embedded link will take people to your plastic duck website page. *Beware: Don't always use the same key words copy for the link if you can. Mix it up a bit or simply use your domain name.*

How the metadata helps: Here's an example of an organic listing of a website. The text in bold shows searched-for key words by someone wanting to find legal help on healthcare, that is, "**legal, advice on healthcare in New York.**"

Legal Advice on **healthcare** | Crimeandpunishment & Co | **New York**
  https://crimeandpunishment.com/**healthcare**
  We offer first-class **legal advice. Healthcare** specialists, with over twenty years' experience in the health and care sector, we're here to support, protect and give sound legal advice to you. Based in New York, call us today for a fee free, no obligation chat.

Here you can see how an organic search listing is made up of the:

- Page title
- Website address (URL)
- The metadata description with all the vital search words/terms included

A "responsive" website: For many years, a website has been designed to be viewed on a desktop computer. Not so now. More and more of us are making use of time away from our desks to read and search for content. All good and knowledgeable website developers will ensure that your website is responsive and can be viewed on a smart phone and tablet screen as well. If you are not sure whether your current website is responsive, you can check by simply searching for your site on your phone and/or tablet. It the design doesn't adjust to fit the screen, if parts are missing or text isn't easy to see or disappears off the page, chances are it's not responsive. Take note: In their drive to give their searchers the best experience, Google is now actively downgrading unresponsive websites.

By 2020, smartphones will make up 50 percent of all global devices.
—Cisco.com

SSL Certificate: Vital if you sell online (e-commerce) to encrypt financial information and becoming more important even if you do not. Having an ***https://*** before your website address shows that you take security seriously and are professional about looking after your site visitors' information. It is quite possible that websites not seen as secure with an https:// will be downgraded by search engines.

What's Valuable?

Key words in internal anchor text: Within your site, internal anchor text helps your visitors navigate around. For example, "You'll find more about our plastic ducks on our bath time fun page." Just ensure that the text around the link is natural and reads well.

Key words in the <alt> tags of your images: Although spiders can't see your pictures, they do read the <alt> tag description of it. Use your key words within these descriptions. This is also necessary for screen readers used by the visually impaired.

Key words at the start of your copy: Still keeping it natural and well written, if you can use your key words early on, it is valuable for SEO.

Metadata description: Entered via your CMS, the metadata description can currently be around 230 characters long. A well-crafted description is valuable because search engine users see it in search result listings as the description of your particular website page. Within it you can not only use your key words that people are searching for, but can also use as little free marketing message as in the example above.

Links from directories: Links to your website from high-traffic, relevant directories can help boost your rankings. *But beware: Having hundreds from just any old directory can harm your site ranking, so be choosy—keep up the quality.*

A sitemap: Check your developer has included a sitemap on your website and ensure it is up to date. This helps visitors and spiders move around and find things easily on your website.

What's Good?

Key word font: Similar to key words in headings, if your key words are in a larger font or bold, it makes them stand out as more important within the copy.

Key words in your metadata: Entered via your CMS, Google is reportedly going off these, but it doesn't hurt to add them in if there is a box to do so.

Hyphenated URLs (web addresses): Using hyphens in your URL or web address makes it easier for the spiders to read. For example, www.bathtimebubbles.co.uk/plastic-ducks—this applies to your main domain name too.

Big sites: Larger websites with lots of unique and relevant pages of content are more attractive to people and spiders. In this way, look to develop and segment your content into different "specialism" pages. Depending on what you are selling, group products together and give them a page if appropriate—help your visitor make choices and introduce tantalizing cross-selling opportunities.

Understanding how search engine spiders "read": Spiders also are not schooled in grammar and don't take any notice of punctuation.

That is to say that full stops, commas, semicolons, and the like don't bother them; their job is to pinpoint searched-for words and links. This gives you a little more wiggle room when crafting your text and can help smooth out "lumpy" sentences. As with this example:

We offer colorful, non-toxic, high-quality plastic ducks, for bath time fun. Based in Boston, we manufacture, package and fulfill all our orders from our family business.

In this way, key search words including **non-toxic, plastic ducks; bath time, fun,** and **Boston** will be easily identified by the spiders and you haven't compromised the sense of what you are saying.

Finally, what are the main areas that can positively damage your website rankings? We've taken a look at what's hot; well, here's what's not.

Inadequate design and coding: A poor-looking, difficult-to-navigate, and badly coded site means predictably poor results. Invest as much as you can in a well-developed and designed website, created by a specialist.

Not updating your website with fresh content: Humans and spiders will eventually lose interest and stay away.

Replicating others' content on your site: Simply reusing content from other sites "downgrades" your site because the content is not unique. If the material is under copyright, and you are using it without permission, you are acting illegally; you could be barred from search engines among other more painful things.

Poor inbound links: If the sites linking to yours are from poor sites, unrelated, or inappropriate, this will reflect badly on your site and your rankings.

Not enough text: Lots of big images and little or no text—you've got to give everyone something to go on!

Key word "stuffing": Beware if your key word density goes over 10 percent on any page. If it does, you are deemed to be shoving in your key words too liberally and not writing good, naturally flowing copy and you'll be penalized for it.

Flash: It is now falling out of use for building websites largely because search engine spiders cannot read and index pages built with Flash software. It's also not readable for humans on tablets or smart phones. If you use it for an animation, give it a text description. If you do use Flash, check with your web developer about appropriate HTML versions of the Flash content. Whatever you do, don't use Flash for the bulk of your home page; you'll be making it invisible to lots of visitors.

Broken links: Pages that are not working and show 404 errors, also password-protected areas, are inaccessible to spiders and therefore won't help SEO.

Unresponsive: Your website cannot be read properly on a smart phone or tablet.

Lack of SSL Certificate: Especially if you are an online seller.

And lastly,

Videos and podcasts: These are very useful content marketing tools and are becoming more and more popular as an effective way to share content. However, as with images, search engine spiders cannot index them and therefore will ignore them. So, you may think you have bags of great content on your site but the spiders may beg to differ. To get around this, post the script of your podcast or a breakdown of the main points of the video content on a sub-page within your website linked from your video/podcast and you will maximize the usefulness of *all* your content and it will be indexed and help boost your rankings.

Authentic, valuable information is what people and search engines want. The use of key word stuffing or irrelevant link-building is poor practice, and ultimately, trying to fool the search engines is self-defeating, because not only will they suss you out quickly as a site unworthy of good organic ranking, any site visitors will quickly make that judgment too. Your business and brand are damaged as a result, so what exactly have you gained?

Last but not least, review and amend

It is important to regularly review search engine results and rankings. Nothing stands still; search engines regularly refine the way their spiders perform searches and what they deem as important and valuable for websites. You might hear or read about Google's algorithms—known to us lesser mortals as the complex way in which Google adjusts how its search engine spiders rank sites. If they decide to make a change, you may see your rankings alter. Search engines are constantly seeking great, unique content for their searchers, so give it to them, backed up by a responsive website, good SEO practices, and appropriate security, and your site will do well.

It's also worth remembering that changes in rankings do take time once you have made an adjustment. Posting and updating the content on your site will, however, mean the spiders return more often—another way to give your site the best possible chance of a high organic ranking position.

Pop-Ups for Sign-Ups?

Some content publishers are keen on pop-ups (boxes that suddenly appear without warning when you are reading a section of copy) as a way of driving better conversion rates for sign-up and data capture. They are used because they can be highly successful, but a word to the wise: In the wrong place, pop-ups can be really irritating and it's important to question what they say about your content, brand behavior, and customer service before you unleash them on unsuspecting site visitors. Some security software will automatically block pop-ups too and that's worth bearing in mind.

The Mood Killer

You walk into a shop that looks like it's got some interesting stock. As soon as you put your foot over the threshold, an assistant looms up right in front of your face and demands loudly that you sign up for all the latest offers.

A) How would this make you feel?
B) What would you do?

My answers would be (A) affronted and (B) mutter an excuse and leave as soon as I was out of the assistant's eye line.

Pop-up boxes that suddenly appear, obscuring the text I'm reading and asking me to give my details there and then, I find a huge turn-off. Usually I haven't read enough of the text to make up my mind if I want to receive more information and the appearance of these boxes is annoying and I usually bale out. **Be wary, this way of encouraging engagement can contradict the point of good content marketing.**

If you offer good content and promote your site well and across different platforms, your engagement and visitor sign-up will come and, in all likelihood, will stick.

Your relationship with your site visitor is the most important thing. If you feel that you definitely need a pop-up, create one that works on a delay, so that it doesn't arrive on screen the moment your visitor does— and do offer an obvious "exit" option, so that they can close it just as quickly if they are not interested. Also, think about the following.

Alternative Options to the Pop-Up

Create an attractive and obvious sign-up button or panel that takes your visitors to your sign-up form and put it on the page where it's going to get the most attention from your reader. These include:

- Top of your right-hand-side bar if your site is set up that way. It's the natural place for visitors to look for sign-up offers.
- At the end of your content, article, or blog post. If your visitor has read to the end, they are engaged and you should ask them for action there and then.
- In the footer of your website page—see above!
- Check your website analytics to find out what your most popular pages are. Use this information to decide where to put your sign-up link— don't miss out on this traffic.

CHAPTER 19

Social Media

Social media describes the diverse and growing range of Internet-based platforms, networks, and applications (apps) that all offer a way for everyone with access to create, share, and exchange ideas and information.

Social media is democratic; it allows everyone a way to get their message out into the public domain. It offers us the ability to freely publish our content, and precisely because of this unlimited freedom, there is, sadly, plenty that is poor, unprofessional, somewhat dodgy, and highly undesirable. Yet, there is also a wealth of well-written and curated resources, offering us a dynamic range of personal and business opportunities to learn from and engage with others.

Everything connects . . .
—Leonardo da Vinci

A rich mix of sourcing, recommending, promoting, exchanging, and learning, with social media the more you put in, the more you get out. But how?

Good content marketing through social media is a mindset, and it works best when it is engaging and also solving a problem.

Remember Chapter 7, where we looked at what makes us share? Making people feel **special, intelligent,** and **loved**, giving them content offers:

Value—informative, opinion changing, useful
Currency—newsworthy, trending, influencing
Story—inspiration, vision, ideas, journey
Emotion—desire, joy, relief, envy, fear, humor

Simply thinking that trotting out sales messages on social media will engage your customer and boost your sales is misguided. It may help a little, but it's not the way to use the media. What will work far better is helping your customer solve his or her problems. This will engage their interest, trust, and buying power.

A well-built, -designed, and -written website is important and deserves prioritizing as your online, digital hub. The sharing of online content—ideas, referrals, reviews and news—is also an important part of content marketing strategy. You won't need, want, or have the time to use *all* the platforms available. Your core customer is the same and will have chosen one or two to concentrate on, and from your initial profiling we looked at in Chapter 4, you should know which ones and aim to use those channels.

Your messages need to revolve around the ways that you can help that customer feel informed and solve their problems, even ones they may not even know they have.

For example, let's say you produce and sell memory foam pillows and mattresses. You want to attract customers who have trouble sleeping. Take a look at the following examples of the same Twitter message:

> *Buy now—memory foam pillows and mattresses, competitive prices! www.sleepyhedz.biz*
>
> *10 ways to get a good night sleep—free guide to restful nights and great good morningswww.sleepyhedz.biz*

Which message is more appealing? Which offers a solution to a problem and shows expertise? Which can lead to a sale from someone who didn't even know that they could benefit from foam pillows and mattresses?

Make your customer feel special, intelligent, and loved. How about two more different tweets on a similar theme?

> *Carrots—overstocked—2 for 1 offer, today only. www.madcarrots.com*
>
> *Succulent, only 41 kcals per 100g, negligible fat and no cholesterol—go crazy for carrots—2 for 1 today. wwwmadcarrots.com*

More and more today, social media gives people options; they don't want to be told what to do. They want to learn, to feel intelligent and special, and to make their own informed buying decisions.

Rapper Kanye West possibly said it best in his tweet: "Don't ever try to sell me on anything. Give me ALL the information and I'll make my own decision." Thank you, Kanye.

Think like your customer. Change their behavior with your content marketing and create a customer for life. But how long does it take?

Social media is a marathon, not a sprint. Think how long it takes to meet a new person; get to know them, get to know what they stand for and how they behave. And then how long does it take for you to feel confident enough to lend them any money?

The building of trust and lasting relationships takes time.

If, through your content, you can confidently answer the question, "Why should my core customer engage with me rather than someone else?" then, more often than not, they will.

Deceptively, social media tools appear to be free to use, but don't be fooled—they are not.

They cost you your time and that is a very precious commodity for owner managers and busy businesspeople. No one wants to be a busy fool. The balance between what you want to do and what you can manage in terms of your content marketing is crucial. Whether you take on the responsibility or delegate it to a member of your team, you need to plan carefully and then make use of these undoubtedly good social resources to benefit your business in a strategic way. This will ensure that you don't waste your time.

Having identified how your core customer likes to hear about, share, and learn things discussed in Chapter 4, you're clear that your role is to build engagement by helping them solve problems that, in some cases, they didn't even know they had. Now you're in a good position to plan your social media strategy alongside your more traditional marketing activity. We're going to take a look at the most popular social media platforms and channels that will be of greater or lesser use to you in your content marketing strategy.

Blogs

People enjoy finding like-minds, swapping information, sharing a joke, learning new stuff, and getting ideas. Ultimately this kind of activity leads to trust, and trust, as we all know, can lead to all sorts of exciting possibilities.

*B2B companies that blog actively generate 67% more leads
per month than those that do not.*

—Socialmediab2b.com

What Are They?

Back in 2004, blogs, the nickname given to "weblogs," really began to gain ground as a mass participation medium; in other words, a way for anyone and everyone to talk about what interested, annoyed, upset, or otherwise enthused them. With the added benefit of search engines checking out the blogs for links and key words, it soon became apparent that blogs were going to be a really useful way for individuals, organizations, and brands to raise their online profiles.

Why Use Them?

As we know, in business, trust is intangible, yet trust is a key element of any negotiation or sale, as opposed to blind faith, which can get us into all sorts of trouble. A blog is a great way to give your business personality and help establish brand behavior, but also lay the groundwork for showing your current and potential customers how you can help them through your expertise, what you stand for, and your methods, ideas, and advice on a whole range of useful information, all with the view of ultimately convincing your customer that they should trust and buy from you in a market teeming with competitors.

Well-written and consistently delivered, a blog will also improve your search engine rankings and you'll be easier to find online by people searching for information on your expertise.

Here's a breakdown of getting the most from your blog:

1. **Host your blog on your website, not an independent platform**
   If this is your business's blog, get it on your website. This will focus your online activity and website traffic in one place and avoid splintering your online audience.

2. **Include key words and phrases that you have identified for your website**
   Use the key words that you have identified for your website within your blogs in the title and early on for added SEO brownie points.

3. **Appreciate that this is a way to engage and share with others; be generous**
   Your blog may be read by colleagues, customers, fellow industry professionals, potential customers, casual "drop-ins," and competitors.

4. **Set out your goals for your blog**
   This may be to increase enquiries, website traffic, and, possibly less easy to measure, better brand awareness. Plan your blogs, their timing, and content. Watch the analytic statistics of your website.

5. **Join the dots: Align your blogs with your overall marketing strategy**
   Tie it in with events and activities coming up in your business calendar. Within your blog you can show market intelligence by anticipating change and comment on current development. Highlight events or activities your business is engaged in, including corporate social responsibility (CSR) and work in your community, which is a great trust builder. React to relevant news. Your opinion could soon be valued.

6. **Don't overdo it, but do it regularly**
   Consistency is important. Make producing your blog manageable by involving others. If you do, make sure you edit them to keep the right "tone of voice." Don't ramble on forever and remember it's a public forum for your brand—give it personality but don't get personal.

7. **Be informative, honest, and generous**
   Offer experience, ideas, links, values, and announcements, making your blog attractive and worth returning to (this doesn't exclude fun stuff—share the joy!).

8. **Understand that a blog is an investment and part of your long-term content marketing strategy**

   Random and irrelevant blogs are a waste of time and effort. They won't build the engagement you're looking for.

9. **Make it a two-way street**

   Encourage feedback and comment. It's really valuable and you'll learn about what your customer likes and is looking for.

10. **Guest blogging**

    This is a good way to expand your reach by blogging on other sites, such as your partners' websites and industry forums. Be generous; invite other experts you respect in your field to guest blog on your site; it will all build your profile as an expert in your field. Consider inviting a member of staff to blog—though you'll edit it. They could talk about their responsibilities, work with clients, the latest regulations, and/or new projects, for example.

11. **Acknowledge the possibilities**

    As your blog archive builds, you may find that there is a book emerging or wider recognition of your expertise within a sector. A good way to collate your amassed business knowledge—be alive to any new opportunities that your blog may bring!

12. **Finally, enjoy developing a "voice" for your business**

    A style that is more informal than other channels you may be using.

Together with more traditional elements, a blog can be a highly effective tool, offering a good way to reach out to the most important people in the life of your business—your core customer.

Joining the dots: When putting together a great blog, check:

- What makes us share?—Chapter 7
- Successful copywriting starts here—Chapter 12
- Press releases and how to write a headline—Chapter 14
- Testimonials—Chapter 20
- Spit 'n' polish—error-free zone—Chapter 21
- Ideas factory—Chapter 22
- LET YOUR CONTENT DO ITS JOB—
- where can I SHARE?

*Signpost to it from Twitter, LinkedIn, or a Facebook page. Post on
your website; could it form a press release in its own right? How
about the beginnings of a book or wider guide on your sector or
industry?*

Webcasts, Webinars, and Podcasts

What Are They?

A webcast is the term given to broadcasting over the Internet; where
an organization can "live stream" or deliver audio and video content to
people with an Internet connection, so the webcaster will have many
simultaneous listeners or viewers. Businesses and public organizations also
make use of this technology to deliver training programs, council meetings, conferences, etc. One of the first webcasts was from the Macintosh
New York Music Festival involving Apple in 1995.

A **webinar** comes from combining website and seminar. Participants
just need a computer with access to the Internet and speakers or head-
phones. Webinars are useful for training, as, delivered live, they have an
interactive element that webcasts don't offer. A live webinar can require
pre-registration and begin on a set day at a set time. Your site visitors can
not only watch and listen, but also message and/or speak to you as you
give your workshop. Webinars may also be simply "on demand" previ-
ously recorded and usually, but not always, requiring your visitor to sign
up to be given access, and in this way you can capture your visitors' data
to engage with them further.

The **podcast** has been with us now for over a decade. The term generally describes a downloadable audio file from a website, and with the
rise of the smart phone, if your core customer doesn't or can't always
be in front of a screen, podcasts are a good way to deliver valuable
content. Today, you'll find over a millions podcasts available, from
repeated radio shows to lectures, storytelling, and business content
such as training guides. Check out platforms like SoundCloud and
Apple iTunes.

Why Use Them?

The webinar offers businesses a very useful online tool. Live or recorded, webinars can be a great way to deliver content directly to interested participants' computer screens, informing your customer, building trust, and reinforcing your brand credentials. They enable you to offer a personal touch and increase your website visitors' knowledge. Uses may include:

- "How-to" guide
- Product use instructions
- New product or service introduction
- Sharing of expertise
- History of a company
- Internal training/information

Within a webinar you present visual and audio material. Predominantly a narration over a series of slides, video, and/or animation, to illustrate your topic, you can also employ some attractive and well-designed infographics to help make your point. As you are not there in person to deliver your presentation, it is very important to deliver good slides, as these are all your website visitor will have to look at while listening to your commentary. The slides need to follow a structured flow and also look visually appealing and engaging.

There is a range of businesses offering straightforward ways to set up webinars and you can create them yourself by using free online meeting software, including Open Meetings.[1] Paid-for webinar services are also available, including the likes of Adobe,[2] which also offers a free trial period so that you can have a play.

---

[1] Open Meetings: free webinar resources, discover more at: http://openmeetings .apache.org; other resources are available!

[2] Adobe webinar resources, discover more at: http://www.adobe.com/uk/products/ adobeconnect/webinars.html; other resources are available!

Here's a quick rundown of what to consider when you are thinking about putting together a webinar:

- Plan your webinar with an introduction, the main elements, and a summary to round off your topic.
- First let your participants know how the webinar will work and what to do if they want to ask a question.
- Introduce your presenter or presenters within the slides: their role and experience.
- Deliver your introduction and overview of the topic.
- Deliver the main elements of your topic. If it is a live webinar and you want to offer your participants time to ask questions, insert a slide to let them know that you will wait to take questions at that point before moving on. It's good to also reassure them that you will respect their privacy and when answering a question you won't reveal their name or business, so that no one gets put off.
- When you have given a final summary covering your points, your final slide needs to thank your participants and tell them what actions they can take next. This could be to indicate further resources to help them and ways to get in touch with you. Ask for feedback from participants to help you gauge how effective and useful it is: Was it useful? Would they share it? What else might they want to know?

Whatever you do, please *don't bore* your audience with an unrelenting parade of bullet points. Use pictures and graphics and themes to help get across your points. Animate your slides to achieve a smoother presentation, but be aware that too much animation may make the slides slow to load on computers with lower broadband speeds and cause problems for some participants.

A podcast isn't interactive, unlike a webinar, yet it is a very neat way to deliver information, guidance, and opinion in regular and easy-to-consume chunks.

The biggest benefit for a consumer, apart from the content, is being able to choose exactly when and where they listen. This may be happily tucked up in bed, on a long car journey, or during the morning commute. If you like the sound of creating downloadable audio to build your audience, podcasts are well worth investigating. Podcast uses may include:

- "How-to" guides
- Information for the visually impaired
- Lectures and speeches
- Interviews with sector specialists
- Industry/sector updates
- Product or service information
- Regular comment and opinion
- Stories

Lots and lots of podcasts out there are waiting to be downloaded, together with a range of online tools to help you get started, which include www.audioboo. This UK-based website and hosting platform for podcasts offers bags of information and guidance on how to get heard. Here's a short breakdown of things you should consider:

- Listen to others podcasts, including those of your competitors, and learn from them.
- Think about your core customer first and foremost—this isn't about what appeals to you.
- Include a sign-off (possibly your strapline if appropriate) and your website details for further engagement.
- Keep it simple—don't overdo the sound effects; the point is valuable content delivered in a professional way.
- Make sure you don't include any material that isn't yours or that isn't royalty free—copyright rules still apply.
- Don't turn it into an advert, remember you're sharing.
- Invest in a good microphone—poor production will devalue your brand and what you have to say.
- People enjoy natural conversations—think about inviting guests on or hosting "guest podcasts" of sector specialists.
- *Always* plan, practice, and review—use online analytics to track the performance of your podcast.

- Be regular and consistent across all your content production.
- Create a podcast name, description, and summary—to encourage people to click on to it. Add your logo to look professional.
- Similar to using video and the platform YouTube, discussed later in this chapter, ensure that you can take full advantage of your content by placing a text version of your podcast script on your website, possibly within a blog, so that you don't miss out on SEO content (see Chapter 18).

Joining the dots: When putting together a great webinar or podcast, check:

- What makes us share?—Chapter 7
- Spit 'n' polish—error-free zone—Chapter 21
- Ideas factory—Chapter 22
- LET YOUR CONTENT DO ITS JOB—where can I SHARE?

Signpost to it from Twitter, LinkedIn, your blogs, or a Facebook page. Promote it via your website and don't forget your email footer too!

A Word to the Wise

Find webinars and podcasts that you like. Check out their length, style, content, and production values. Do a "dummy run" and, if in doubt, take professional advice. Poor quality of content and presentation will only undermine your efforts, brand, and customer trust.

Social Media Platforms—Make It Relevant, Keep It Current

Let's take a look at some of the most current and popular social media platforms for B2B and B2C.

These brief overviews are not intended to be chapter and verse on social media platforms that are continually evolving, along with the swelling ranks of their fans and followers. What I hope they will give you is an insight into how applicable they may be to your business and some basic dos and don'ts on how to make the most of them. Tackling them in alphabetical order.

LinkedIn (www.linkedin.com)

What Is It?

When people search for you online, what do you want them to find? LinkedIn gives you a free and detailed personal platform on which to detail your professional career, together with additional pages for your business and products or services.

Launched in 2003 to connect professionals and B2B online, LinkedIn is an easy way to curate and update your professional details, untied to specific businesses or jobs. You can build your profile to include your career progression, skills, awards, and interests and, importantly, to create a database of LinkedIn contacts. These connections can endorse and recommend you for your expertise and you can share the love by endorsing and recommending your trusted colleagues and associates too.

It's your platform to sell yourself and you're in good company. In 2016 LinkedIn had around 530 million users in over 200 countries and territories, speaking 20 languages. It's currently "the" online professional forum. If you are a professional and do not have a LinkedIn profile, most people will wonder why not.

When someone puts your name into a search engine, and not your business, your LinkedIn profile link will pop up. The basic platform is free to join and allows you to find and be found by fellow professionals, colleagues, and associates and "connect" with them. When you are connected to a fellow LinkedIn member, they will be able to receive your posts or updates and you will see theirs, as well as viewing their full profile. A paid-for premium account will allow you to send messages to those you are not connected with, see who's been checking out your profile, and refine your searches to target specific types of people and more.

Why Use It?

LinkedIn is a good forum to keep all your professional information in one place and up to date. It's also a good signposting tool for delivering content to your B2B contacts. You can post short updates or write longer articles as little or as often on your LinkedIn account as you like. You can also like, share, and comment on the posts and articles of your contacts that will appear within your "news feed."

You can create a separate page for your business or company, together with product and showcase pages, delivering specific content, including videos and promotions. Those that work with you in the business can also feature on a company page. You can also follow other companies to receive their updates.

You can set up your own or join a special interest group. These groups are a good way to join in conversations, ask questions, and show expertise by answering questions and commenting. The range of groups is extremely broad, covering all industry sectors, for example, independent publishing, environmental issues, HR, coaching, construction, and advertising—another good way to signpost people to more detailed content on your business website or blog.

How can LinkedIn help your content marketing? Here are some quick dos and don'ts to help you get the most from your LinkedIn profile:

Do:
1. **Use key words and phrases within your copy**. The copy you use on LinkedIn is searchable by the search engine spiders, just like your website.
2. **Ensure you have your website address, blog, and Twitter feed filled in on your profile**. When you post updates and longer articles, you should also try to use your key words and phrases and include a link to your website. These updates may highlight a recent blog, press release, new appointment, an event you are attending, or a resource. Longer articles are a way to show greater expertise and opinion and influence others. In turn, your connections can share, like, or comment, drawing even more attention to your profile and the content you are signposting and sharing.
3. **Check out the different professional interest groups**. These focus attention on different aspects of business. Look for the groups where your expertise will be welcomed and join in the conversations.

4. **Set up a company page for your business**, from which you can promote content on and about your products and services. LinkedIn members can follow your company page and will receive your company update posts.

5. **Give recommendations to those suppliers and colleagues you have enjoyed working with and endorse them for their skills.** They are very likely to return the favor when appropriate and this all builds up your profile and helps make the decision to choose you over your competitor an easier one.

6. **Post regularly and engage with others**.

Some Mistakes to Avoid

Don't:

1. **Leave your photo blank**—it looks like you can't be bothered. Also, don't be tempted to use a holiday snap; a picture of you with a pet, child, or relative; a "glamour" headshot; or one from 20 years ago. Use a clear, well-taken headshot of the approachable professional you are.

2. **Forget to post**. Remember the SEO value of your profile and post content that includes your key words. You are getting exposure among your contacts, and if shared, liked, or commented on, their contacts too.

3. **Forget to respond to people who would like to connect, ask a question, or endorse your skills**. A "thank you" goes a long, long way.

4. **Forget it's also a great place to look for staff and suppliers** for your business.

5. **Ignore the availability of the company** pages and opportunities to grow your followers, post further content, including videos, pictures, and more.

Bear in Mind

LinkedIn begins with a **personal profile**. If you have a number of staff who are members, they are first and foremost representing themselves but also representing your business. So, it's wise to get together to discuss the best practices of using LinkedIn and how your business is being discussed. Offering a professionally taken headshot for them to include on their profile is a good way to create goodwill and cohesion, and comes back to the consistency of brand behavior. If not you, designate a team member to run your LinkedIn company page who is completely in tune with how you see your brand behavior and development.

The entry level is free; an upgraded or paid Premium Account includes in-depth metrics; thus ways to identify and filter sales leads through more company information, view people outside your network, and more. It's also worth noting that you can export the name and email address of your LinkedIn connections, which can enhance your direct email database and extend your reach. *As the method to do this seems to alter, as with many of the social media platforms, my solution is to simply do an Internet search for the latest "how to guide" and you'll find the most up-to-date information.*

Comparable to Facebook's ability to home in on your key target audience, you can opt to create and use paid advertising at a budget you set and target segmented industry professionals by pay per click or pay per impression of your post. If you have a company page, LinkedIn's Sponsored InMail offers you a way to reach professionals beyond your page followers, sponsoring your content, as opposed to a straight advertisement, to any segment of LinkedIn's premium account holders based on their profile data.

Joining the dots: Let your content do its job. *LinkedIn is a highly visible and trusted social media platform, so make sure you insert a link to your LinkedIn account at the footer of your emails, on your website, and on other social media platforms. The easier you make engagement, the more people will engage with you, and find and read your content. When you post on LinkedIn, think about where else you can share the content, including Google+ and Facebook, and signpost it with a tweet . . .*

Twitter (www.twitter.com)

What Is It?

A social, B2C and B2B, platform, launched in 2006, Twitter is a "micro blog" that enables users to send initially 140-character and more recently 280-character text-based messages called "tweets." Your text tweet can also include a link to a web page, blog, photograph, video, or PDF. People interested in you can follow or subscribe to your Twitter account. You can also comment on and quote other people's tweets.

In the same way, you can sign up to follow other people. As a follower you can read what people tweet, share, or retweet; reply to them; and send direct messages that are not viewable publicly.

In 2012 this social networking platform was passing the 500 million followers mark and rising. Jack Dorsey, the man behind the idea, said of the name: "We came across the word 'twitter' and it was just perfect. The definition was 'a short burst of inconsequential information,' and 'chirps from birds'. And that's exactly what the product was."

Today, what started off as "inconsequential information" has grown into a dynamic global tool. From the sublime to the ridiculous, tweeters include movie stars, scientists, the Dalai Lama, U.S. presidents, NASA, and the Anchor Butter cow.

Why Use It?

Brands, entrepreneurs, and the well-known quickly spotted the opportunity of attracting more followers to increase engagement and sales by applying their brand behavior to Twitter. It's a global sound bite and signpost to content to create loyal followers, alter consumer behavior, and increase sales.

In this way you can see how a brand that understands its core customers' needs, wants, and wish list can use social media as a vehicle to channel traffic to its website, where it can publish and promote valuable information consistently, becoming a resource, an influencer, and a trusted supplier of goods. Businesses can also pay to create sponsored or promoted tweets. These are marked as such and enable brands to target users outside their immediate followers.

But just as there are many examples of how brands can be smart and use social media to enhance their image, it needs to be remembered that social media is a two-way street.

If your customer has a complaint about your product or service, their complaints can be aired far and wide, damaging your brand's reputation. Everyone makes mistakes and the key to limiting the damage is swift engagement, responding to someone's concerns or comments as soon as possible with a reasonable solution.

A colleague of mine recently received very poor service while traveling with a national train operator. He tweeted about his bad experience as he traveled. Within 5 minutes the train company in question had responded to his tweet, publicly apologizing and telling him they would be looking into his issues. This was the right way to respond, achieving good PR in the tone and speed of their reply. My friend was pleasantly surprised that they were listening and psychologically it made the uncomfortable journey a little less irritating. And what we are discussing now is not their poor service but their prompt response to a problem—job done.

When you have a conversation with someone, you do expect (quite reasonably) some reaction or response. So, if you make Twitter part of your content marketing strategy, you need to be prepared to tweet and respond regularly and consistently; otherwise your efforts are wasted and your business and brand appears untrustworthy.

How can Twitter help your content marketing? Here are some quick dos and don'ts to help you get the most from your tweets:

Do:
1. **Follow others first**. See how they do it; check out who they follow, and how often and what kind of content they promote. Do this with competitors and people you admire and dislike. It will help you work out your own Twitter strategy.
2. **Fill in your biography** (make it about benefits to your customers rather than your mission statement) and location, with a link to your business website and post up a professional picture of yourself, or your logo. Social media promotes a personal approach and many feel that headshots, not logos, are better for engagement.
3. **Be yourself**. Even tweeting as a representative of a brand, you need personality. If you are delegating this to a member of your team, discuss the tone of your tweets and the goal of stimulating clicks through to your website and/or blogs. As with all your content marketing, it needs to be aligned with your overall marketing strategy.

Understanding how it all joins up is essential to help focus followers on your blog, website, video guides, Facebook page, etc.

4. **Share valuable content**, including pictures and video; make it meaningful and retweet (RT) similar good content for your followers. You are the expert in your business and marketplace; use that to good effect.

5. **When you can, thank those that retweet (RT) your tweets.**

6. **Respond promptly to a direct or private tweet**/message and keep it private. In other words, don't make a conversation public that didn't start that way.

7. **Use a hashtag (#)** to highlight specialist areas in your tweets, for example, #sales, #HR, #ethics, #Xmas #Austria. These hash-tagged words act like neon signs—*they are great* for allowing people who are already on the lookout for valuable content on a particular subject to find you. So, do a little research on useful hashtags and include them with your tweets when you can, but don't be too prescriptive. Mix it up a bit.

8. **Use pictures:** *Fact*—using pictures in tweets attracts more attention and interest. Tweets with pictures get more attention and engagement than those without. The URL for your picture won't count in your 280 characters, so there's no reason not to use one.

9. **"Like"** tweets by clicking on the heart icon. This gives those you follow a warm glow and, more importantly, an idea of the content you appreciate. In the same way when one of your followers likes a particular tweet of yours, take note—your followers are telling you what they want.

10. **Use a URL-shortening tool such as Bit.ly** to automatically shorten long website addresses. This gives you more characters to use for comment.

11. **Link your Twitter account** to your Instagram account if you decide to use one.

12. **Use a scheduling tool such as TweetDeck® or HootSuite®** to schedule tweets for when you cannot be in front of your screen or on your mobile device. Sending tweets at different times of day may attract more attention depending on your core customer profile. Also, as people dip in and out of the platform throughout the day, it's worth rewording the same message and sending it out a couple of times.

13. **Feel comfortable in establishing your own style, aligned with your brand behavior:** remember consistency and value always.

Ninety-two percent of retweets are earned by 'interesting content.'
—Mindjumpers

Some Mistakes to Avoid

Don't:

1. **Leave your profile blank or scantily filled in**. This sends out a poor signal to customers immediately. Concentrate on the benefits to your customers, not your mission statement.
2. **Ignore direct tweets** or those that retweet (RT) your content.
3. **Overplan your tweets** so that you don't react to everyday events and issues within your industry.
4. **Moan**. Apart from the odd burst of righteous indignation, don't do it; it's deeply unattractive.
5. **Always feel you need to use a hashtag (#).**
6. **Always be selling**; people will switch off.
7. **Tweet lots then do nothing**. Know your capacity, plan your time, and stick to what you can manage.
8. **Use capital letters unless you** MEAN TO SHOUT.
9. **Worry about unfollowing people.** They are not alerted.
10. **Retweet someone else's content and then forget to acknowledge them**—it's bad manners.
11. **Get anxious that you've missed out on something** or someone has missed your tweet. Because you aim to be regular and consistent, your followers will grow.
12. **Forget to check your spelling**. Mistakes make you look sloppy.
13. **Ignore all the wonderful content and resources that you are being offered**. Follow people, learn from them; this will help you spread your message and content to places you thought you'd never reach.

If you are interested in particular customers/competitors/associates/experts and what they are saying, you can create a list, including on it only those tweeters you want to listen to. These lists may be public or private. If they are public, then the tweeter will be notified that they are on your list. If you make the list private—for your own personal research—they will not know that they are on it. Some businesses create lists to bring together people with common interests and needs. In this way they can listen, share and collaborate more easily.

It is also possible to embed your Twitter timeline into your website pages, so that visitors to your site can see your tweets and any retweets or responses. It's a good way to keep your website looking current and show real-time engagement, delivery of content, and your ability to be an up-to-date, responsive expert in your field.

For more advanced fine-tuning there are online tools that give you the ability to analyze who is following you and which of your tweets are the most popular. In this way you can work to improve your reach.

Advertising on Twitter

You can set a budget to promote an account, a single tweet, or a subject that is trending, denoted by a hashtag, for example, #sausages. Promotional tweets encourage engagement and from those that are most likely to be interested. In the same way you would pay Google when someone clicks on your advert, your business will pay a fee when someone follows your promotional account. All sponsored tweets are marked as "promoted" so that people can tell what is and is not paid for content.

You'll find these mini ads turning up in the organic listings—the "Who to follow" suggestions in your account, and also in trending lists using hashtags.

Twitter offers help guides on how to set up advertising accounts and analyze the results. If your key audience lives and breathes Twitter, this is where you need to be. Visit: https://business.twitter.com

Joining the dots: Let your content do its job. *Promote your Twitter account. Email your database and invite them to follow you. Add a "Tweet" button to your website, email footer, and blogs to encourage your site visitors to share your content with their followers. Add your Twitter name and logo to your business card, brochure, and printed literature.*

Facebook (www.facebook.com)

What Is It?

Facebook was conceived and created in a Harvard University student dorm by Mark Zuckerberg (current CEO), Eduardo Saverin, Andrew McCollum, Dustin Moskovitz, and Chris Hughes. Founded in 2004 as an online "getting to know you" website for Harvard's students, as of late 2017, with an annual income in the billions of dollars and over 2.7 billion[3] MAUs (monthly active users), Facebook is a social phenomenon and it holds a lot of information about an awful lot of people.

Facebook has become popular because it fulfills a basic human need; people love to keep in touch and share stuff that they care about. What matters to them matters to their family, friends, and colleagues, whether that's holiday snaps, a great restaurant recommendation, new job, or birthday celebration. It's a highly personal platform for users and offers advertisers tantalizing rewards of access to millions of consumers who are already signed-up members of the "I love to share" club.

Why Use It?

By users choosing to share information about themselves on Facebook, including age, gender, location, and interests, advertisers can benefit by homing in on their target market much more quickly, such as: men over 40 who like gardening and live in Florida, or young women aged 18 to 25 who like keeping fit, giving to charity, going to gigs, and who live in Washington. Website developers have also clambered on board, helping their business clients by creating and building applications (apps) that integrate with Facebook to help them reach, engage, and influence users through competitions and special offers.

Further to personal pages, by creating a page for your business on Facebook you can introduce another platform for your customers to see and share your content. Used as a dynamic signpost similar to Twitter, yet

---

[3]Forbes. 2017. "Global 2000: Growth Champions." http://www.forbes.com/companies/facebook/

having the ability to deliver more words, pictures, and video, Facebook can be a potent generator of traffic to your website.

If your key core customer is active on Facebook, it's time for you to take a closer look. Before you can create your business page you will be required to first create a personal page—you may already have one.

How can Facebook help your content marketing? Here are some quick dos and don'ts to help you get the most from Facebook:

Do:
1. **Fill in your profile or "about us" section fully**, using the key words you identified for your website. This will help people find you if they are doing a search. And ensure that you put in all contact details, your website address, and physical address for the "place" section if you want to attract people to your shop or business.

2. **Promote your page.** Email your current database and invite them to visit and "like" your new business page. Place a link to your Facebook page on your website and at the footer of your emails and have the Facebook URL on your printed literature, including your business card. If you have a personal Facebook page, invite your friends to like your business page and share with their friends to help you spread the word. Put copy at the bottom of your invoices, inviting your customers to like your page and take up exclusive Facebook offers (just remember to create some!).

3. **Experiment with what time you post and what kind of content you offer**, for example, opinion and comment, offers, videos, photos, etc. You should have a good idea of what content you need to focus on from understanding your core customer. Monitor what prompts your customers to actively "like" and "follow" your content and page. When someone "follows" your page, they may see your updates in their news feed; when someone hits the "like" button, they are enjoying what you're offering and they will also automatically see your posts in their news feed and you'll be in front of them more often. **Check back with Chapter 7 and what makes us share.**

4. **Decide how you can encourage more "likes" and "follows."** How about sharing a free "how-to" guide, articles on your area of expertise, an exclusive offer, or a discount?

5. **Ask for feedback and opinion.** Setting up online chat or a website forum can be expensive, yet Facebook offers you a free "talking shop." Always ensure you respond swiftly to queries or complaints to underline your customer care credentials.

6. **Add in Facebook user names of your clients and suppliers into your posts** (e.g., @NewYorkLaundry); they will be notified and hopefully follow your page back and mention your services in return.

7. **Play with hashtags (#).** Similar to Twitter you can currently add a hashtag to a word in your post, for example, "#kids" if you are, say, selling children's clothing. When someone puts #kids into the search bar of Facebook, your post will come up along with a stream of other posts all on the subject of kids, such as kids' games, food, clothing, ideas for holidays, etc. Research what might work well for you.

8. **Link your Facebook account up to your Instagram account**, if you choose to have one.

9. **Have more than one administrator or manager** for your business page who is able to post and respond to questions and queries if you are not able to check into the page as often as you would like.

10. **Tie your activity in with your overall content marketing strategy** and other social media activity to keep information "joined up," such as promoting blogs, events, articles, guides, webinars, offers, and competitions. It will help to **diary it** regularly each week.

11. **Check how you're doing by monitoring.** At the time of going to press, you need 30 likes to give you access to the Insights section of your business page. Insights will give you statistics on the reach of your posts. If you choose to take up paid advertising, this section will also give you stats on your paid ads. Facebook is also testing a star rating and review section— time will tell if this sticks around—the jury is out on whether it will be effective or indeed helpful.

56% of customers say that they are more likely to recommend a business or brand after becoming a fan.
—Social Media Today

Some Mistakes to Avoid

Don't:

1. **Forget your brand**—your business page needs to reflect the look and feel of your brand and your website. As well as being consistent in tone of voice, visually you need to reassure your customer that they have arrived at the right place. Ensure your logo is loaded up correctly and think how the larger cover image can be used to show off what you do. Be aware Facebook doesn't like CTAs such as discount promotions or website URLs on the cover image. Check out businesses you admire and your competitors to see what they are doing.

2. **Give it the hard sell**. This is a highly social sharing platform for engagement and fun with some serious thought behind it.

3. **Miss out on website traffic** by linking your Facebook ad back to your Facebook page. If you choose to use Facebook ads, link them to your website where you are in full control and can offer customers far greater content, make more varied CTAs, and have the opportunity to capture their contact details.

4. **Post the "same old, same old"**—vary your content and you'll keep your customers interested in what you have to say and offer. Again, check back in with Chapter 7 on what makes people share and Chapter 22 on how to come up with content ideas. This includes being generous and sharing content of other business pages that you "like" and follow.

5. **Ignore the many tools Facebook can offer**. Investigate the ways you can get in front of more people who may be interested in you and take some time to explore the apps you can choose to use on your page, including video, Twitter, and Instagram. Facebook has a comprehensive online "help" and "how-to" series of guides to help you.

6. **Forget to stay professional**, but be human.

7. **Use a "click farm"**—what do I mean?

When someone "likes" your page they form a link with you and when you post information, a comment, or a picture, the person who has liked your page will receive it in their Facebook newsfeed. Some business pages have hundreds and some have thousands of likes. Large brands, as you may expect, can have a fairly enthusiastic following, while others present more of a mystery—they must be doing something great to get such a lot of likes, right?

Interestingly, all is not often what it seems and likes can be manipulated for the cost of a few pounds or dollars paid to a "click farm," which exploits cheap labor and the availability of the Internet. Click farms set up false accounts to create hundreds of thousands of fake likes for their clients. Many people look at the number of likes to judge the quality of a page and before they make a purchase, which means click farms could play a significant role in misleading people. Not only do these click farms present a challenge for businesses and Facebook itself, which encourage the use of "likes" as a reliable metric, but they are also potentially breaking the law in misleading individual consumers.

Put aside vanity and be authentic. Create good content and offer real advantages to your page fans and you'll have a far clearer picture of your customer and their needs. After all, this *is* the point.

Advertising on Facebook—"Boost Your Posts"

Using all the collated data of its active users, Facebook makes its vast wealth from advertising to them. You can use its might in targeted adverts to users you believe will be interested in what you have to say, using gender, location, hobbies, likes, etc. If your customer loves Facebook, then these paid-for messages can complement your content. For up-to-date information on promoting your posts, increasing your likes, and targeted advertising, visit: www.facebook.com/advertising

Joining the dots: Let your content do its job. *Promote your Facebook business page. Email your database and invite them to follow you. Add the logo to your website, email footer, and blogs to encourage your site visitors to visit; "like" your page and share your content with their followers. Add the Facebook logo to your business card, brochure, and printed literature.*

Google+ (www.google.com)

What Is It?

Google+ was launched in 2011 with a lot of fanfare, but over the years has not found the foothold it perhaps expected as a social media player.

In its current form it is pretty much the domain of adults, attracting less young/teen attention. It is a good way to push out your content but also, and perhaps more importantly for you, it will help support your Google organic search rankings. In other words, it can help move you up the search listings. It appears to be a widely accepted truth that Google more favorably ranks websites connected to Google+ accounts than those on other social media platforms. Let's face it, why wouldn't they?

You will need a Google account to create a Google+ account and, similar to Facebook, there are personal pages, business (or brand) pages, and the opportunity to promote or sponsor posts. The platform has found its advocates, but it has not matched the stellar success of Facebook in terms of monthly users.

Why Use It?

Google+ is another platform to publish and share your content. Its particular attraction is largely in support of your website rankings, which is pretty good reason all on its own. You can organize your followers into groups or "circles." You post content into your "stream" and your followers can see it, or you can make it public. You will also see the content from the people you follow. As a Google+ account holder, the main tools you may use currently include:

Google Circles (professional or social) is a way to share your content with people or communities that will be more interested in it, instead of pushing it out to a wider, but possibly less focused audience.

Google Hangouts offers video chat and instant messaging and can be used for up to 10 users.

Google+ Local has replaced Google Places as the location information for your business and helps rank websites in a given locality for the searcher.

Brand Pages are for your company information and posts giving you the opportunity to showcase your business.

Google+ Communities is for ongoing conversations on particular topics.

Google+ also makes use of the hashtag (#) way of signposting to specific content as with Twitter, Facebook, Pinterest, Instagram, etc., so bear in mind what key words you can use with a hashtag to highlight your content to searchers.

Your Google+ profile may also be connected to Google AdSense should you be using this Google paid advertising tool to promote your business.

Joining the dots: Let your content do its job.

In terms of the dos and don'ts, Google+ is very similar to its competitor, Facebook. The key is relevant, valuable, and shareable content that drives your followers to your website.

Keep watching and listening to what the search giant is up to. Google are never ones to let the grass grow under their feet, so keep an eye on their new ideas and initiatives and don't miss out on a tool that may be just right for your business promotion. Check out https://support.google .com for information, guides, and forum support.

YouTube (www.youtube.com)

What Is It?

Launched in 2005 and owned by Google since 2006, YouTube has 1 billion users, that's nudging one-third of the Internet onboard.[4] Not all just cats freaking out over cucumbers (no really, take a look), YouTube is a search engine in its own right and a superb free resource giving you the ability to broadcast to the world by uploading videos to showcase your products and services. Watchers of your videos can subscribe to your channel, so they are alerted when you post up new material. They can also like, comment, and share your material.

---

[4]YouTube. 2017. "YouTube by the Numbers." https://www.youtube.com/yt/about/ press/

Why Use It?

A very useful tool, YouTube gives you the ability to create your own channel on which to post videos and webinars. Importantly, you can then also give them a home on your website. Once a video is uploaded to your YouTube channel, their software can generate a code that, once placed or "embedded" in your website, will "stream" or display your video, as and when a visitor lands on your webpage. This means you don't need large amounts of bandwidth for your website and you won't incur a big annual hosting bill. You can also switch them on and off as you wish.

Videos are highly effective content *if* you have a goal and understand how they can align within your marketing strategy, *and* they are well produced. All the same rules apply to video content as to written copy: value, consistency, quality. Don't let a poorly executed video damage your brand. If you are considering creating videos for your business and you don't have the expertise, seek the right professional help to produce what will attract and inform your customer.

How can YouTube help your content marketing? Here are some quick dos and don'ts to help you get the most from YouTube.

First of all here are some ideas for the kinds of video that might work well for your product or service:

- Tutorials on a particular product's use
- Overview of services/product lines
- "How-to" guide—can apply to almost any discipline
- Background story on a brand or journey of a business
- Regular "vlog" spot
- Interviews with clients—testimonials
- Seasonal videos, for example, holiday messages
- Story behind a particular product or service
- Building/moving to new premises and meet the team
- CSR and work in the community
- Fund raising for greater awareness of your business presence
- Animation, a fun and different way to show off your expertise

Do:

1. **Use your business branding** to help your customers know they are in the right place.
2. **Add subtitles** to your videos to help your visitors.
3. **Use your key words** in the descriptions of your videos. These are crawled by the search engine spiders and use the "tags" to help searchers find your content. There is a YouTube key word tool to help you.
4. **Embed your videos within your website** and promote across you Facebook page and your other channels.
5. **Use hashtags (#)** to signpost searchers to your content, for example, "#innovation."
6. **Make sure your website link is in your profile description.**
7. **Be creative.**
8. **Be consistent.**

Some Mistakes to Avoid

Don't:

Forget to promote your YouTube channel to your customers and across your other social media platforms and on your printed marketing material.

Forget to respond to comments or queries on your YouTube channel—it's all about encouraging engagement.

Think that a very obviously homemade, wobbly, badly lit video with a poorly groomed presenter, who is clearly reading their words off a sheet of paper, is going to look OK. A substandard video reflects directly on your brand.

Imagine that your content will immediately "go viral" (shared by those not directly following you by lots and lots of shares). In all probability it won't; it takes time, timing, luck, and innovation—but you never know!

Advertising on YouTube

Similar to Facebook you can drill down into gender, location, age, and interests to get your content in front of potentially interested customers.

You pay a fee when someone decides to click on your video, and analytics will show you who you're reaching, when, and on what, that is, computer, tablet, smart phone. If your core customer loves their YouTube then this is where you need to shine. For more information on advertising on YouTube, visit: https://www.youtube.com/yt/advertise/

Joining the dots: Let your content do its job. *Promote your YouTube channel via Twitter, LinkedIn, and Facebook if you use them. Make your email recipients aware of your latest video in your email footer and highlight it in a newsletter. If it's a big feature of delivering your content, then ensure you regularly get the message out on all your available platforms.*

Instagram (www.instagram.com)

What Is It?

A mashup of the words "instant" and "telegram," and developed for mobile devices, Instagram was launched in October 2010 as a purely photo-sharing platform. Today, you can use it across all mobile and desktops, and video has been added as an option along with a range of filters to enhance your photography. You can "geotag" your photo to a location and users are encouraged to use hashtags to define the photo— both for location and for what's happening. The key is relevant and specific, for example, #Florida #lakeside #picnic. Viewers also have the ability to zoom in and out of a photo to see more detail by "pinching" the screen. Users can also bookmark favorites and create collections.

Why Use It?

Simple is always best and Instagram is a wonderfully simple idea. You capture a moment and you share it. The ease of joining in, and following others or themes that you like, has seen this social platform rocket in popularity. It is a good way for a business to create a real sense of personality, especially if it has plenty of scope for visuals, such as an outdoor events company. In actual fact Instagram can be used to great effect across all types of sectors, including construction, entertainment, education, engineering, agriculture. You name it and there will be a picture that can go with it. Instagram is also integrated into Facebook. Once you have linked the accounts you can also choose to share on Facebook when you share a photo or video on Instagram.

How can Instagram help your content marketing? Here are a few tips to help you get the most from Instagram:

1. Use your direct work email address.
2. Once you have set up your account, choose a good user name that reflects your business name or what you do.
3. Fill out your bio, fully including your website address—this is the only place on Instagram that you'll be allowed to use it as a clickable link, so don't forget to fill it in.
4. Choose an eye-catching and relevant profile picture as this will appear with all your photos. Make it different. If it's you logo photograph, stick it on a mug, a tree, your cat—get creative!
5. Set up your social sharing and link your Twitter and Facebook accounts with it, so that your content can reach further!
6. Follow others first. What are you competitors doing? Do it better.
7. Use the hashtags: Check out the popular ones and the more niche to see what could work for you.
8. Don't be afraid to experiment and have fun!

Lastly, don't ask people to follow you until you have got some photos to show them!

Advertising on Instagram

To reach more of your key audience, you can create little adverts for your business by promoting a post. Similar to Facebook you can select the type of people you're looking for, and where and how much you wish to spend. For further information, visit https://business.instagram.com/advertising

Joining the dots: Let your content do its job. *Promote your Instagram feed. Add the logo to your website, email footer, and blogs to encourage your site visitors to visit; follow and share your pictures. Add the Instagram logo to your business card, brochure, and printed literature, even the side of your van.*

Link your Instagram account up to your Twitter and Facebook page to further promote the content you create.

Pinterest (www.pinterest.com)

What Is It?

Launched in 2010, Pinterest is all about sharing photos, images, and artwork, and now videos and gifs (short animated or video clips). Content that shows graphically what you love and, importantly for business, what you do. The fastest website ever to achieve 10 million unique visitors. In October 2012 Pinterest launched business accounts and by 2013 Pinterest pages offered business owners the ability to include the prices of products and even recipe ingredients and predominately attracts the lifestyle, homestyle, cooking, craft, and fashion sectors

Why Use It?

If you sell or create stuff around the lifestyle sectors, get onboard by opening a free business account. The site gives you the ability to "pin" up pictures, images, graphics, videos, and gifs onto virtual "boards" that reflect subject themes; others can then "re-pin" and share your content on their own boards. A virtual scrapbook, also popular among Pinterest communities is giving board space to influencers, in other words, "other stuff we love," as, with all social media, it's about liking, commenting, and sharing others' content as well as your own.

This way of collating and curating content is very useful for driving traffic back to your website because when you pin up content, your followers are able to read a description and find a link to your website.

How can Pinterest help your content marketing? Here are some quick tips to help you get the most from Pinterest:

1. Brand your page with your logo and fill in your profile.
2. Descriptions are spidered by search engines, so use your key words where you can; also use hashtag words, as with Twitter, Facebook, Google+, and Instagram.
3. Beware of infringing another's copyright when you pin—read the rules and always acknowledge your sources.

4. Add a watermark to protect your original pins. Relatively easy to do; there are "how to" blogs and tutorials a brief "search" away.

5. Infographics work well on Pinterest and this is a great way to share complex information and show off your expertise.

6. Add a "pin" button to your website and make it easy for your website visitors to pin up your content on their boards.

7. Don't forget, Pinterest can host videos too!

8. Always try to thank "re-pinners"—remember this is engagement not direct selling.

Advertising on Pinterest

As with Twitter and Facebook, you can also deploy "promoted pins" on Pinterest to better target your core customers, and if this is where your customers like to find their inspiration and ideas, be there for them. Find out more at www.https://business.pinterest.com/

Joining the dots: Let your content do its job. *Promote your Pinterest boards via Twitter, LinkedIn, and Facebook if you use them. Make your email recipients aware of your pins via your email footer and highlight it in a news-letter. If it's a big feature of delivering your content then ensure you regularly get the message out on all your available platforms.*

And there's more, lots more. More platforms and more ways to engage will continue to be developed. Some will capture the popular imagination while others will fade away. On each of the platforms I've looked at in this book there are already improvements in the pipeline, as the software developers try out new ideas and ways to capture atten-tion, attract advertising, and achieve global domination. My advice is stay curious. Be alive to the way the world learns and shares and, most impor-tantly, the evolving tastes of your core customer. Be where they are and match your content to what they're looking for.

The Long and Short of It (Part 2—Social Media)

Following our look at long and short copy in Chapter 9, here is a breakdown of the ideal, or optimum length of online content for attracting attention. Thanks to Kevan Lee for his blog *The Optimal Length for Every Social Media Update and More* published on the social media blog Buffer Social[5]:

Domain name = 8 characters
Tweet = 71 to 100 characters
Facebook post = 40 characters
#Hashtags = 6 characters
Google+ headline = 60 characters
Width of a paragraph = 40–55 characters
Email subject line = 28–39 characters
Headline length = 6 words (this is particularly tricky to achieve!)
Blog post = 1,000–1,600 words
LinkedIn posts = 25 words
YouTube video = 3–3½ minutes
Podcast = 22 minutes
TED Talk = 18 minutes
Slideshare = 6 minutes
Online seminar = 18 minutes

A useful guide, these statistics do not, however, tell us about the quality of the content. So, don't get too hung up on the numbers; where content marketing is concerned it should always be about well-written, valuable content, not word count. Be it headlines, articles, blogs, or videos—their length should be determined by what it takes to attract, engage, and inform, and no more.

Measuring the Results of Online Content Marketing

Content marketing, especially delivered through social media, is a long game, and the building of a loyal core of super fans won't happen overnight. In some cases your content immediately ignites your customers' imagination to the extent that it spreads rapidly out into the wider public domain and goes viral. The viral effect, however, is as elusive as it

---

[5]K. Lee. 2016. "Infographic: The Optimal Length for Every Social Media and More." https://blog.bufferapp.com/optimal-length-social-media

is capricious and the process of marketing your services and products through consistently delivering quality content is an effective but longer term reality.

Analytics software on your website, most often based around the free tool Google Analytics, can tell you where your traffic is coming from and that will include your social media referral sites. Email marketing software analytics can also link up with your social media platforms to help you track and monitor uptake of your content and what is popular with your core customer and wider audience.

It's important to monitor your website and social media traffic on a regular basis.

Regular monitoring will teach you which blog posts are being responded to and shared, which photos are most popular, and/or which Facebook posts, videos, and tweets are shared. This will begin to build a picture of where you need to place your efforts, extend the reach of your content, and attract more customers, likes, subscribers, and followers. Finally,

All roads lead to Rome, in other words, everybody's heading to your website.

Email marketing and the social media I have outlined will give you a sense of which ones may work best in signposting and helping to deliver your content strategy. Being in the places where your customer likes to learn about and share information is vital to extending your reach and engagement, be that guest blogging, creating articles for online industry forums, and/or appearing on your partners' websites. *But* just as "all roads lead to Rome" (apparently), ultimately all your online content and signposting should lead to your website. Similar to the marketing email, some are hailing the death of the website. Not so, it's your online home and it's going to be for the foreseeable future.

If your visitor arrives at a website that is poorly designed, written, and maintained, you have just blown the credibility you were so carefully building. You have wasted their time and they will be less inclined to make a repeat visit. First things first; get an interesting, current, and well-populated website up and running, and as you develop content for it, bring in the appropriate social media strands to support it and your business.

CHAPTER 20

Testimonials

For printed or online content the testimonial is one of your best marketing tools. When it comes to a reassuring presence on a website, within brochures, or on professional forums like LinkedIn, there is nothing better. Real recommendations; great little adverts for your products and services, where are yours?

If you are one of the many businesses that collect them lovingly in a file, only to be seen by a tiny percentage of your potential customers, if at all, you are not alone.

Possibly offending our naturally modest sensibilities, it may feel a bit like showing off, yet if someone has taken the time and effort to put together good words about what you do, it seems churlish not to use them, especially as they offer a unique differential between you and your competitors.

Top Tips for Testimonials

- Talk to your clients about the work you do with them—how do they feel? What else can you do to help them? And ASK for a short testimonial and let them know how it will be used.
- Seed them appropriately across your website and promotional material.
- Show those relevant to the content you are delivering.
- Use "pull quotes" (eye-catching short excerpts taken from the full testimonial). Not sure how? Here's an example: "Believe me, you won't find a finer widget . . ." taken from: "I've bought from Acme Widgets for 3 years. Unfailingly professional and high quality, believe me, you won't find a finer widget in the North." Lisa Renault, Twine Engineering

- Always attribute testimonials for authenticity (see above).
- Update them.
- Importantly, ensure your client is happy for you to publish their words within online and printed material.
- Reciprocate—do your bit and cement good business relationships by giving testimonials to your suppliers.

Finally, it can be difficult to ask for testimonials. Let's face it, it is not always an easy thing to do; people are busy and they forget to respond, even if they are initially enthusiastic. If you feel awkward, ask a member of your team or commission a copywriter to contact your customers on your behalf. They can talk to your clients for 5 minutes and get enough information to craft and get sign-off on a great testimonial for use across your printed and online content.

Isn't it about time you learned how to take a compliment?

CHAPTER 21

Spit 'n' Polish

It may feel like you've done the job when you have finished writing a piece of copy, but if you haven't edited it, redrafted and edited it again, proofread and reproofed, you're only half way there.

I saw the angel in the marble and carved until I set him free.
—Michelangelo

Editing

There are two phases to creating a piece of copy: the writing stage and the editing stage. They should be separate.

Editing means taking your first draft and refining it until it really works as a quality piece of content that will do the job you need it to. It is the process that ensures your material has the right structure: introduction, main body, and summary or conclusion. It is your "sense check" to eliminate repetition, hyperbole, or waffle and it precedes proofreading, the process to pick up typos and spelling errors (see my later chapter on proofreading and use of synonyms).

Edit Checks

1. Does it make sense? Information and comment following in the right order?
2. Does it do the job? Check in with your wider marketing/content strategy and AIDEA; check back with Chapter 12 for a recap.
3. Could ease of reading be helped by shorter sentences, subheadings, and/or more paragraphs?
4. Weed out repetition and unnecessary words and phrases.

5. Have you got the tone and style right for your key customer?
6. Is the title compelling enough?
7. Is the CTA clear enough?
8. Use the Flesch Reading Ease stats to check readability. See Chapter 18 for a reminder on readability tools.
9. Proofread for errors of grammar, typos, and spelling mistakes.

A common error I often come across is the business talking about itself first and the benefits of its products or services second. To counter this, keep asking yourself, is this what my core customer wants to know or is it what I want to tell them? If it's the latter, start again.

As you edit you may also alter your headline or title, because in writing you have discovered a far more compelling line to use, as discussed in "How to Write a Headline" in Chapter 14.

Unless you are constrained by a rigid word count limit, like Twitter at one end of the scale and a longer advertorial or web page feature at the other, only go on for as long as it takes to make your point and no longer. Length depends on who will be reading it, how, where, and what you want to get out of it. As we discussed earlier in Chapter 9, "The Long and Short of It," your copy should be "fit for purpose," giving your readers what's required and no more.

Your first edit should be the most drastic in terms of amendment, and subsequent edits should refine your work further. Whatever your intended final word count, writing too much is better than writing too little. If you have not written enough, it may mean that after editing you are trying to think up some more angles or ideas. In general you should work on an average of four to five edits or drafts in order to get your copy right.

One of the hardest things to do in an edit of your own work is take out bits that you find amusing and intellectual or where you have shown off with a bit of a flourish.

Even when it breaks your egocentric little scribbler's heart, kill your darlings.
—Stephen King

Self-indulgence sneaks up on you. As soon as you feel yourself verging on the smug, carefully cut and paste out your favorite lines into a new document for personal enjoyment later and get on with your job.

Flex Your Editing Muscles

Make editing a habit and build up your editing muscle. Like most things, the more you practice, the better you become. Whatever the copy, check in mentally with your content marketing strategy each time and you'll go a long way to ensuring that all your content is consistent with your brand behavior and delivering your key messages: valuable, easy to read, well-presented, and welcomed. All the things your customer wants and your competitors will envy.

Proofreading

"The fourth book in the trilogy . . ."

Yes, this really appeared on a hardback book dust jacket. This mistake got past the author, his editor, a subeditor, and numerous publishing executives. It was eventually spotted by a designer, but, alas, too late to prevent the junking of a 30,000 print run of lovingly created covers.

If you are asking for people's trust, don't erode it with errors. Typos, spelling mistakes, repetition, and glaring grammatical errors all tell your customer about your attention to detail—or lack of it. The professionalism of your copy is judged not just on its content value, but also on the number of errors it contains. When you publish *anything*—a tweet, a LinkedIn post, a comment on Facebook, right up to a 50-page client proposal—there is no acceptable level for errors. Yes, they happen, right under the noses of professionals and I'm no exception, "Even monkeys fall out of trees,"[1] but it's zero tolerance time, people.

---

[1] Japanese proverb.

How to Spot Errors?

1. If you are using a word-processing software, make use of your spell/ grammar checker first. Make your amendments, then **print out** a copy of your work and set it aside. *Computer spelling and grammar checkers are handy but you have a far greater vocabulary than your computer, so, do not rely on it—it won't pick up 100 percent of errors such as typos, hyphenations, correctly spelt words in the wrong place, and misused and/or missing words. It also can't do calculations or check numbers.*

2. Wait a few hours or, more usefully, the next day before you reread your work. Checking it over too quickly means there is a good chance you'll be reading what you "think" you've written, rather than reading what's actually there and thus spotting errors.

3. Get rid of any distractions. If you are thinking of other things, or surrounded by noise and bustle, you will not be able to concentrate fully on the copy. Proofing requires concentration.

4. Decide if you are using the accepted English or American spelling of words. It is your choice but you must be consistent.

5. Read your work aloud. It is amazing how much this helps, especially for improvement of punctuation and picking up any missing words.

6. Keep your place with a ruler to ensure you do not skip any lines. If you leave your work, mark the place you got up to clearly and you'll start at the right place on your return.

7. Keep a dictionary or thesaurus handy—if in doubt, **look it up**.

8. Mark any corrections with a colored pen and/or highlighter. This will make them much easier to pick out and you'll be less likely to miss any when retyping.

9. Recheck those numbers. Add up forward then backward to confirm totals, while also checking for any misplaced decimal points and commas.

10. Read your copy backward. Yep, sounds odd, but this will really help you spot any spelling mistakes; it is too easy to start "reading" the copy, instead of "proofreading" it.

11. If your copy is lengthy, with many pages, rest your eyes every 15 minutes or so. This will give your eyes and brain a break, helping to keep you focused on the job.
12. Finally, when you feel sure you have found all the errors, pass the copy to a colleague. Nine times out of ten they will spot something you missed.

Track Changes and Proofreading Symbols

Today, many people use the immensely useful Track Changes to amend and proofread documents, while some do still employ handwritten proofreading symbols. If someone is proofreading your work on paper and not on screen, it's worth taking time to understand the marks and symbols they are going to use. Check with them on their system, so that there is as little room for misinterpretation and time wasting as possible.

Common Mistakes and Misconceptions

When we put pen to paper in business, first and foremost we want to be easily understood. Keeping it simple is best to help ensure our readers completely understand what we are saying. Perfect punctuation may be desirable, but I believe that as long as your reader understands the sense of what you are saying and you are consistent in your approach, you can't go too far wrong. *But* there are a small yet resilient bunch of grammatical errors and misconceptions that do hamper understanding and show a lack of attention to detail. The following are probably the worst offenders, though you may have your own pet hates:

A) **"Its and it's"**

"It's" with an apostrophe is simply a shortened form of "it is" or "it has," for example, "It's too late to proof that proposal, as it's been posted out." If you are *not* saying "it is" or "it has," then you simply use "its." For example, "When you take away its central column, it collapses."

If you're in any doubt, just read your sentence aloud, in full, and you'll know immediately which version to use (. . . if in company remember: head voice).

B) **The apostrophe to show possession or belonging**

"Our Managing Director's office is on the fourth floor."

Or

"Our client's needs come first."

The examples above give the singular form. *But* be careful; most of us have more than one client, so if you don't want to confuse your readers and leave them wondering which client in particular you favor so highly, the plural form would be: "Our clients' needs come first." Now everybody is happy. If you leave the apostrophe out altogether, you just cause confusion or hilarity. Lynne Truss, in her zero tolerance approach to grammar, *Eats, Shoots & Leaves,*[2] cites some great examples of missing apostrophes, including "Dicks in tray," leaving us all with a highly unfortunate mental image.

C) **"Your" and "you're"**

"Your" describes something belonging to someone. For example, "Your payment details are completely secure." "You're" is simply a shortened form of "you are." For example: "You're entitled to receive our biggest discount." Again, if in doubt say it aloud and in full to know the right one to use.

D) **"Their," "there," and "they're"**

"Their" describes belonging or possession. For example, "Their reaction to the advertising campaign was ecstatic."

"There" describes a sense of place; somewhere that is not here. For example, "Get your booklet from over there." "They're" is simply a shortened form of "they are." For example: "They're ready to host the event tomorrow."

E) **"To," "too," and "two"**

"To" is often used with verbs. For example, "We are happy to meet with you at your offices." It is also a preposition and describes direction. For example, "We work to the very limits of our expertise."

"Too" describes extra or more than needed. For example, "If you have

---

[2]L. Truss. 2003. *Eats, Shoots & Leaves* (London: Profile Books). ISBN 1-86197-6127.

too many conflicting messages you will confuse your customers." "Too" can also be used for "also." For example, "Me too!" "Two" is the number 2, as in "one, two, three . . ."

F) **"Fewer" and "less"**

This is a tricky one. Possibly the easiest way to think of the difference is fewer is to do with individual items that you can count. For example, "There are fewer freelance consultants available today." "Less" is to do with how much and relates to a concept or something you cannot count individually. For example, "We appear to have less operational capacity in this field."

G) **"Affect" and "effect"**

"Affect" is a verb and describes influence or part of a process. For example, "Our poor call handling adversely affects our reputation." "Effect" is a noun and is an outcome or a result. For example, "The effect of greater investment means our call-handling complaints have reduced." *Watch out, "effect" can also be used as a verb meaning "to bring about." For example: "We hope to effect a change in the current regulation."*

H) **"Complement" and "compliment"**

"Complement" is a verb, which describes how two different things go better together. For example, "Our range of leather wallets complements perfectly our luxury luggage collection." "Compliment" is a noun, which means a comment that expresses admiration, approval, or respect. For example, "The compliment paid by our MD to our apprentices was well-deserved."

I) **"E.g." and "i.e."**

"E.g." is used when you are giving an example. It comes from the Latin *exempli gratia*. For example, "We offer a range of garden tools, e.g. spades, forks and clippers. "i.e." is used when you want to say "in other words" or "that is" when you are explaining something and it comes from the Latin *id est*. For example, "We recommend our 'out of the box' pack, i.e. a basic tool kit for the beginner."

J) **"Practice" and "practise"**

"Practice" is a noun and is often used to describe a legal or medical practice. "Practise" is a verb, for example, "To get it right you have to practise."

While this applies to UK English, in American English they don't make this distinction.

K) **"Principal" and "principle"**

"Principal" has a couple of different meanings, as follows: an adjective describing the first in importance, for example, "We consider ourselves the principal partner in this deal." It can be used as a noun describing an amount of money, a debt, on which interest accrues; it also describes the head teacher at a school.

"Principle" is a noun and it describes a code of behavior, a rule, or defines the way in which something works, for example "Archimedes's Principle."

L) **"Stationery" and "stationary"**

"Stationary" describes something that doesn't move. "Stationery" is the term given to pens, paper, colored sticky pads, fluorescent highlighters, envelopes, and all the fun stuff in your office cupboard.

M) **"Organize" and "organise"**

For words ending in "ize" or "ise," the *Oxford English Dictionary* (OED) gives the suffix "ize" first, before "ise," but tells us both are correct. Whichever version you favor, simply be consistent in its use. It's also worth noting that academic writers tend to follow the OED and it is the spelling standard used in style guides for the United Nations (UN), including the World Health Organization (WHO). Other international organizations that prefer "ize" include the International Organization for Standardization (ISO) and the World Trade Organization (WTO).

N) **Hyphenated words**

A hyphen's role is to help make sense of the words for the reader. When trying to figure out when to use them and when not, you will also find conflicting advice and the arguments rumble on. The large majority follow the rule of hyphenating compound adjectives when they come before a noun, for example, well-written copy. The same would apply to compound verbs: word-stuffing or link-building. Your guide should always be sense and consistency. For example, we'll take a sign reportedly seen in a guest house: "Why not take advantage of our trouser repressing service?" Clearly, the landlady has suffered in the past from badly behaved trousers. Swap in "re-pressing" and the offer makes a lot more sense.

"**Up to date**" often used and often confused. Here's a good rule of thumb: if you use the phrase as an adjective, in other words to describe the status of something, for example an up-to-date report then it is hyphenated. For other uses, for example, "get up to date," it is not hyphenated. Another common stumbling block is "**cooperate.**" It's widely accepted that it doesn't need a hyphen. If you prefer to use one, do; just be consistent.

Finally, always try and avoid using a hyphen to split a word over two lines. It's ugly and more importantly slows down the reader making sense of your copy.

O) **CapitaLs within tITles**

Another element of copywriting that often trips people up is the use, or not, of capitals within headlines or titles. If your house style or brand guidelines demand capitals for titles, and some do not for stylistic reasons, here's a quick overview to help you.

Words you *do* capitalize

Adjectives: hopeful, crazy, helpful, big
Nouns: office, woman, keyboard, sale, coat
Pronouns: it, your, you, she, he, him, hers
Verbs: find, buy, enjoy, take, remember
Adverbs: quickly, really, hopefully, locally
Subordinating conjunctions: that, because, as, when, where

Words you *don't* capitalize

Prepositions: to, by, on, from, at, with, via, of
Articles: a, the, an
Coordinating conjunctions: and, or, for, in, but

Repeating Repetitions

Finally, **remember the use of synonyms** to help you write more interesting content. Synonyms is the term given to words that are the same or have a similar meaning, for example:

fast: prompt

know-how: expertise

graceful: elegant

answer: solution

knowledge: experience

big: large

spacious: roomy

luxury: quality

cheap: cost-effective

brief: succinct

snug: cosy

handmade: artisan

Using synonyms gives you lots of ways to be creative, keep your reader interested, and get your message across. Have a thesaurus handy for this purpose. A useful online resource to help you find and use different words is The Visual Thesaurus (www.visualthesaurus.com).

Having input the word you want to begin your search with, this website graphically displays a range of similar-meaning words, which quickly allows you to pick out and follow different avenues of thought to give you inspiration. The site requires a small annual sign-up fee but you are offered a number of free trials to have a play first. If you enjoy writing and word play, the site also offers lots of helpful articles, information, and guides.

CHAPTER 22

Ideas Factory

Looking for an idea for a blog, newsletter, or campaign? We are all mulling, dissecting, worrying, and looking for ideas, so where are they, how do we find them, and how do we ensure our creative juices don't dry up?

Logic will get you from A to B. Imagination can take you everywhere.
—Albert Einstein

"There's nothing new under the sun." King Solomon reputedly made this remark, and in essence it's true, but don't let his rather pessimistic, if accurate, forecast put you off; we have something Solomon didn't: We have an overwhelming abundance of ready information.

Never in the history of mankind have we had access to such vast quantities of opinion, data, news, reportage—call it what you like, we are bombarded by it and what makes the difference for us is our take on it; our ability to shape, extrapolate, or look at it in our own unique way spawns ideas and innovation.

Look up from your keyboard, desk, or (if you're not feeling so great) the floor and listen to the ideas that are literally walking, talking, and being published all around us. This insight, combined with more computing power in our pockets than sent the first men to the moon, means we have no excuses for an apologetic look when it comes to creating content.

Ideas Are Walking and Talking All Around Us

Listen to your customer. Listen to your colleagues, partners, and associates. Listen to wider world changes, innovations, and trends. Take notes. Think about it. Write about it.

People are telling us what they want all the time, all around us. It's well worth talking less and listening more. And originality? That is yours. Your voice and message to inform, sell, and inspire others; enough for them to wonder where you get all your good ideas from.

CHAPTER 23

Que?

The Internet has gifted us the ability to speak to people in countries all over the globe. Our websites are visited, accidentally or on purpose, by people from many different nations, cultures, and languages. So, with the potential for new markets opening up, if you are thinking of selling your products and services abroad, you may be thinking of how you can translate your copy into another language.

Language is wonderful: words with multiple meanings, regional expressions, or turns of phrase, slang and local sayings—all there to trip us up. If you are considering turning your carefully crafted product manuals, instructions, printed material, and web copy into another language that you are not fully familiar with, look for good advice and work with a reputable translation agency that employs native speakers.

> *In which language do you think?*
> —Swiss census form, 2001

Google Translate, useful as it is for single words and short phrases, cannot take into account figures of speech or a particular industry or sector's way of talking about what they offer. Don't be tempted to translate paragraphs of your scintillating copy into another language this way; if you do, you'll be heading for an embarrassing disaster.

Differences in meanings can be extremely funny, but they can also be worryingly confusing and sometimes offensive, so you need to do all you can to mitigate the risk of misunderstandings and damage to your brand.

Quirky, funny, and bizarre mistranslations gathered from around the world litter the Internet; here are just a few bizarre and daft examples that I have spotted in various blogs and posts:

Swiss restaurant: *Our wines leave you nothing to hope for.*

Danish airline: *We take your bags and send them in all directions.*

Bangkok temple: *It is forbidden to enter a woman even a foreigner if dressed as a man.*

Doctor's office, Rome: *Specialist in women and other diseases.*

Budapest zoo: *Please do not feed the animals. If you have any suitable food, give it to the guard on duty.*

Car rental instructions, Tokyo: *When passenger of foot heave in sight, tootle the horn. Trumpet him melodiously at first, but if he still obstacles your passage then tootle him with vigor.*

If others grapple this helplessly with our language then you can be sure we're failing just as spectacularly with theirs, so it pays to hire the best help you can. To help find the right professional translation service, start with the American Translators Association (ATA; www.atanet.org).

CHAPTER 24

Briefing a Copywriter

To help you initially create and guide your tone and style across your content marketing, ensure content is delivered at particularly busy periods or for special ad hoc projects; very often it pays to bring in a professional copywriter.

> *A professional writer is an amateur who didn't quit.*
> —Richard Bach

A professional copywriter will save you time, no question. They are used to turning around highly effective copy quickly, and because their purpose is to concentrate on producing the words, once briefed you can let them get on with wrestling over straplines, promotions, press releases, and online copy—it is a weight off your mind and your inbox. Not only that, but a good copywriter will be skilled at delivering a well-crafted piece of writing that encompasses everything you want to get over: grabbing the attention, creating interest and desire, qualifying it with evidence, and ensuring clear CTAs.

To enable them to do the best possible job for you, it is important to have a good, honest relationship; how well you work together is part and parcel of producing the best copy. Do they listen? *Really* listen? They should. Listening to what you do, why, and how is vital. They'll need to know all about your brand, company, and team to produce words that speak for and about you in a compelling and engaging way. In this respect, building a relationship with a copywriter pays dividends because after the initial brief and project, subsequent projects take less time and effort on your part as your copywriter can hit the ground running.

When Briefing a Copywriter, What Do They Need to Know?

Scope—a big picture view of your sector, business, and the project in hand. How it fits in with other marketing you are doing, including what you want to produce and the platform you want to use, for example, blog, advertorial, or brochure, etc.

Aims—what you want to get out of it and why.

USPs of what is being sold.

Timescale—when you want the finished copy delivered.

Style—drill down into your brand's tone and style. How do you want to come across to your customer? As I keep repeating, your brand behavior is crucial to building engagement and trust, so your "tone of voice" is just as important. A copywriter can use their experience to establish that for you, for example, professional, straightforward, friendly, welcoming, etc. Or you may already have a house style that your copywriter will want to understand, replicate, and enhance where possible. If in doubt, look at other companies' websites/brochures and decide which styles you like and which you don't.

Everything Matters

When I work with new and long-standing clients, when they ask what I want to know, I always say "everything matters." Even if my client doesn't believe some information is directly related to the job in hand, or their marketing goals, experience has taught me that all information is important. Information about staff, new jobs, community work, innovation, outside interests, and what influences them; stuff that makes them anxious and future plans—it all helps build up a picture of the people and products in the business and a business worth engaging with.

The Drafting Process

Agree when you want to see the first draft with your copywriter and when they deliver; come back to them with feedback. It's rare to hit the nail on the head first time, but it does sometimes happen. Three to five drafts is a fair amount to aim for. The first amendment will be the largest shift and you will refine less and less as you go. Don't, if at all possible, run the drafting stage by committee. As with anything where a group of people get to have a say, it's almost inevitable that messages get watered down, impact is lost, personality is obliterated, and your copywriter will end up being committed to a home for the tragically enfeebled shortly after delivery of their 14th draft.

Words and Pictures

If a design layout is involved for the content, any copywriter worth their salt will also want to work closely with the graphic and/or web designer and vice versa. **Words, colors, layouts, and pictures work best when they work together**. If your "creatives" are working in isolation, 9 times out of 10 it's going to make the process harder and could feel a little like swimming with one arm tied behind your back; it's uncomfortable and inefficient and can lead to disaster. Get them together and share the joy.

CHAPTER 25

A Word about Design

Picture yourself on a country road. You're on holiday and looking for a good activity to while away a few hours. You're open minded and up for fun. You see a sign; it's a little tatty and the paint is peeling. The letters are hand drawn and it's lost a nail at one corner, making it lopsided. It reads Free Range Eggs. How charming, you think, eggs for tea and you're happy to buy half a dozen from the friendly farmer.

Further on down the lane, you come across a very similar sign. It too is a little tatty. In bright pink paint the uneven letters spell out "Flying Lessons—first flight FREE" in childish print. Most, if not all, people would walk away, incredulous that a flying school would use such poor advertising for its business. If that's what the sign looks like, what does the plane look like?

It may be a crude analogy but the flying school's lack of ability to spot such a mismatch in its expertise and branding is not uncommon.

Just Because You Can, It Doesn't Mean You Should

The power and ease of the computer have given us all quick access to design software. The ability to load design software on a PC, however, does not make us all designers.

> *Image and perception help drive value; without an*
> *image there is no perception.*
> —Scott M. Davis

When presenting your business, first impressions are crucial and everything about the design you use should work hard to tell the viewer about your professionalism, your expertise, and customer-facing care.

It should be appropriate for your market; be attractive to your core customer and instill confidence right from the start.

> *The computer is only a smarter form of the pencil.*
> *It is the person operating it who has the ideas and experience.*
> —Ned Hoste, brand director, The Big Ideas Collective

First impressions count; everyone says it because it is true. When it comes to presenting your business it is vitally important that you give the most professional impression possible. Research over the past few decades, conducted by august bodies including The Design Council in the UK and Harvard Business School, among others, show that the business benefits of getting good design integrated into all areas of business thinking and activity can more than double business returns. Your marketing is certainly no exception.

> *Good design is good business.*
> —Thomas Watson, Jr., CEO, IBM

What Is the Use of a Message That Is Ignored or Never Heard?

The earlier designers are involved in your content marketing strategy decisions the more effective that strategy becomes, and it works best when copy and design work together.

Last Words

*Content without copywriting is a waste of good content and copywriting
without content is a waste of good copy.*
—Sonia Simone, www.copyblogger.com

With this overview of content creation and how you can use it within
your content marketing strategy, I hope I have been able to show you how
you can focus on and engage more with the people that matter the most
to your business—your customers. And how, through your expertise, you
will be rewarded with engagement, trust, and sustainable growth.

**There has never been a better time or more ways through which to
connect and share with each other. Your challenge as a business owner
is to work out the best way to get inside your customer's mind. Let
them get to know you. Give them valuable information and shareable
content and help them make good buying choices. They'll remember
you and, as a result, your business will reap the rewards.**

Further Reading

Ogilvy, D. 2009. *Ogilvy on Advertising*. London: Prion (re-printed). ISBN 978-1-85375-615-3

Maslen, A. 2009. *Write to Sell*. London: Marshall Cavendish. ISBN 978-0-462-09975-0

Truss, L. 2003. *Eats, Shoots & Leaves*. London: Profile Books. ISBN 1-86197-6127

Aitchison, J. 1994. *Cassell's Guide to Written English*. London: Cassell & Co. ISBN 0-340-37587-1

Hegarty, J. 2011. *Hegarty on Advertising, Turning Intelligence into Magic*. London: Thames & Hudson. ISBN 978-0-500-51556-3

Berger, J. 2013. *Contagious*. New York: Simon & Schuster. ISBN 978-1-47111-169-3

Steare, R. 2001. *Ethicability, How to Decide What's Right and Find the Courage to Do It*. Fully revised and extended fourth edition. Kemsing: Roger Steare Consulting Ltd. 2011. ISBN 978-0-9552369-5-2

Trott, D. 2009. *Creative Mischief*. London: LOAF Marketing Ltd. ISBN 978-0-9564357-0-5

About the Author

Jacky Fitt, FRSA, born in North London, she studied stage design at the Royal Welsh College of Music and Drama in Cardiff. Her professional work within theater led her to work in TV and film production, including work with David Puttnam, Terence Davies, and Paul Greengrass. Following work with national UK broadcaster ITV, Jacky became a freelance copywriter, establishing Words to Fitt in 2002.

In 2007, Jacky cofounded the Big Ideas Collective with graphic designer Ned Hoste together with the publishing arm the Big Ideas Library in 2013. In 2015, Jacky was invited to speak at TEDx Pocklington, and her first book, *How to Get Inside Someone's Mind and Stay There*, won the Small Business Book Awards, People's Choice for Marketing. In recognition of her work in the environment, Jacky was also awarded the Overall Achiever Award in Yorkshire and the Humber by the Investors in the Environment Scheme. In 2016, Jacky became Digital and Social Editor of the international arts platform daCunha.global.

In 2017, Jacky became a Fellow of the Royal Academy of Arts, Manufacturing and Commerce (FRCA) and, today, Jacky continues to work with clients throughout the UK and abroad, including ghost writing and editing books; producing articles, web copy, and print advertising; helping to build trust, profit, and good business. Jacky is married to Thomas, has two daughters and lives in York, North Yorkshire, UK.

How to Get Inside Someone's Mind and Stay There, was first published in 2014 by the Big Ideas Library and was winner of the People's Choice category for marketing in the 2015 Small Business Book Awards by smallbiztrends.com.

Jacky's editor credits include: *www.howtobegoodat.work* by Professor Roger Steare, FRSA 2018.

I Am Human—30 Mistakes to Success by Martin Johnson 2017

It's Not about the Beard by Tom Fitzsimons 2015

If You're So Clever Why Aren't You Rich? by Elizabeth Ward 2014

ethicability 4th edition by Professor Roger Steare 2011

Find out more about Jacky's work: www.thebigideascollective.com

Twitter: @jackyatbigideas @Wordyfitt

Index

OTHER TITLES IN THE ENTREPRENEURSHIP AND SMALL BUSINESS MANAGEMENT COLLECTION

Scott Shane, Case Western University, *Editor*

- *The Chinese Entrepreneurship Way: A Case Study Approach* by Julia Pérez-Cerezo
- *Enhancing the Managerial DNA of Your Small Business* by Pat Roberson-Saunders, Barron H. Harvey, Philip Fanara, Jr., Gwynette P. Lacy and Pravat Choudhury
- *Five Eyes on the Fence: Protecting the Five Core Capitals of Your Business* by Tony A. Rose
- *Hispanic–Latino Entrepreneurship: Viewpoints of Practitioners* by J. Mark Munoz and Michelle Ingram Spain
- *The Business Wealth Builders: Accelerating Business Growth, Maximizing Profits, and Creating Wealth* by Phil Symchych and Alan Weiss
- *Open Innovation Essentials for Small and Medium Enterprises: A Guide to Help Entrepreneurs in Adopting the Open Innovation Paradigm in Their Business* by Luca Escoffier, Adriano La Vopa, Phyllis Speser, and Daniel Satinsky
- *The Technological Entrepreneur's Playbook* by Ian Chaston
- *Licensing Myths & Mastery: Why Most Ideas Don't Work And What To Do About It* by William S. Seidel
- *Arts and Entrepreneurship* by Mark Munoz
- *The Human Being's Guide to Business Growth: A Simple Process For Unleashing The Power of Your People for Growth* by Gregory Scott Chambers

Announcing the Business Expert Press Digital Library

Concise e-books business students need for classroom and research

This book can also be purchased in an e-book collection by your library as

- *a one-time purchase,*
- *that is owned forever,*
- *allows for simultaneous readers,*
- *has no restrictions on printing, and*
- *can be downloaded as PDFs from within the library community.*

Our digital library collections are a great solution to beat the rising cost of textbooks. E-books can be loaded into their course management systems or onto student's e-book readers.

The **Business Expert Press** digital libraries are very affordable, with no obligation to buy in future years. For more information, please visit **www.businessexpertpress.com/librarians**. To set up a trial in the United States, please contact **sales@businessexpertpress.com**.

www.ingramcontent.com/pod-product-compliance
Lightning Source LLC
Chambersburg PA
CBHW060611210326
41519CB00014B/3631